THE
CAPITAL RAISING
MASTERCLASS
CERTIFICATE

Hosted by

THE

MONEYGAMES

Visit www.TheMoneyGames.com
for dates and locations.

Enclosed are up to $2000 in gift certificates
found at the back of this book!

WHAT PEOPLE ARE SAYING ABOUT *THE FIVE MILLION DOLLAR BOOK*

Stefan is smart beyond his years, and his book is fun to read, informative, AND packed with solid "how to" strategies. *The Five Million Dollar Book* is a must-read for anyone who is serious about creating wealth through real estate investing. Read it, implement it, and you will shave years off your learning curve and make hundreds of thousands more than you would have otherwise.

> DAVE DUBEAU
> PUBLISHER, CANADIANPROFITSTV.COM

Stefan is a real estate pit bull who is dedicated to helping individuals make sound, smart, and profitable investment decisions.

> MATT WOZNIAK
> VERTUITY MORTGAGE

Stefan is very creative and skilled at making any real estate deal successful. He always finds a way to create a win-win situation for everyone. He is a great business partner, and I highly recommend him to anyone looking to add investment real estate to their portfolio!

> MACKENZIE DOVIDIJA
> REAL ESTATE INVESTOR AND JV-PARTNER

I have had the pleasure of doing business with Stefan and his incredible team. Stefan is a very knowledgeable, cooperative, and inspiring person. Deal with him if you want to get things done, and educate yourself along the way.

> EVGUENI ZABOURDAEV
> REAL ESTATE INVESTOR AND JV PARTNER

Every great entrepreneur in history has known how to put Money, People, and Deals together to create wealth. In *The Five Million Dollar Book*, Stefan has captured the mind-set, the process, and the execution that great entrepreneurs have used for centuries.

NELSON CAMP

ALTERNATIVE INVESTOR OF THE YEAR 2012

Stefan's book picks up where most investors quit. It is essential for a serious real estate investor to learn to put Money, People, and Deals together.

MARC MOUSSEAU

CEO OF WHAT REAL ESTATE GURUS DON'T TELL YOU, INC.

Mind-set is everything. Stefan's book will show you how to create a winning mind-set to do as many deals as you want!

SHAUN FURMAN

HOST OF *MILLIONAIRE MENTORS TODAY*, MMT.TV

Joint ventures are one of the most powerful business techniques available today. However, so few people can effectively explain joint ventures to their prospects. Stefan is a master of explaining effective real estate joint ventures and makes the process easy and simple.

SHELLY HAGEN

PRESIDENT OF DI-RAE DEVELOPMENT INC.

The Five Million Dollar Book makes real estate joint ventures simple and easy to understand. A great book for a beginner or advanced investor!

TAHANI ABURANEH

BEST-SELLING AUTHOR OF *REAL ESTATE RICHES*

If you want to start investing in real estate with none of your own money, then this is the book for you!

MARCO SILVESTRI

2012 INVESTOR OF THE YEAR

THE FIVE MILLION DOLLAR BOOK

MONEY PEOPLE DEAL

THE FASTEST WAY TO REAL ESTATE WEALTH

Stefan Aarnio

Clovercroft Publishing

Published by Clovercroft Publishing, Franklin, Tennessee.

Cover Design by Marla Beth Thompson

Interior Design by Suzanne Lawing

Edited by Christy Callahan

Printed in Canada

978-1-942557-68-5

DEDICATION

This book is dedicated to anyone who is passionately pursuing a dream.

The best rewards in life are reserved for those who are bold enough to make a statement.

Respect the grind,

STEFAN AARNIO

CONTENTS

FOREWORD

For centuries, entrepreneurs have taken resources from different sources and have assembled them to create higher value. Great entrepreneurs like Steve Jobs, Henry Ford, and Donald Trump have all understood very clearly how to assemble Money, People, and Deals together. The intellectual value that these men brought to their ventures was so great that they built their businesses by using none of their own money; this is the skill of the entrepreneur and the fastest way to wealth.

Stefan Aarnio has the makings of a great entrepreneur. I met Stefan in July 2012 at a conference in Winnipeg, Manitoba. I could see that Stefan had achieved a great deal of success in real estate in a short period of time. After speaking with Stefan, I was impressed to hear that he had built his business exclusively with real estate joint ventures and that he, like great entrepreneurs before him, understood how to assemble Money, People, and Deals together for profit. I later learned that my initial impression of Stefan was correct because in November of the same year, *Canadian Real Estate Wealth* magazine recognized Stefan as 2012's Joint Venture Partner of the Year!

Having completed over 1,100 real estate deals in my lifetime, I know what it takes to be a successful real estate investor. Success in real estate requires a full understanding of the fundamentals, a winning mind-set and a timely execution of action. Stefan has captured all of the above in *The Five Million Dollar Book*, and I am very pleased to be a part of this body of work.

If you are looking to create wealth in real estate, in the fastest way possible, you are in good hands. I wish you the greatest success on your journey!

RAYMOND AARON
NEW YORK TIMES BEST-SELLING AUTHOR
REAL ESTATE INVESTOR

ACKNOWLEDGMENTS

I would like to thank all of my partners for believing in me. This book is your work as much as it is mine. There is no such thing as a truly self-made man; I am a synthesis of my environment and everyone around me. Without you, none of this is possible. A small pebble rolling down a hill will eventually become an avalanche. You are the force that pushed the first pebble down the hill. Your faith has created my success.

INTRODUCTION—WHY GREED KEEPS MOST PEOPLE FROM GETTING WEALTHY

We all want to be healthy, wealthy, and wise. Unfortunately, everything in life has a price of admission. In some shape or form, we must always pay for the things we want. For our health we must invest our time, focus, and discipline to go the gym and maintain a healthy diet. To be wise, we must invest our time, effort, and energy to study with the wise men and women of the past, present, and future. To be wealthy we must study money, solve problems, and be prepared to share the wealth along the way. Those who fail to pay for success rarely see it.

The Five Million Dollar Book explores the fastest way to real estate Wealth—joint ventures. Joint ventures are a technique few people truly understand. Of course, many of the largest, most successful corporations use joint ventures every day to earn massive profits while most struggling small investors and entrepreneurs have no knowledge of joint ventures. The truth is that most small entrepreneurs and investors are too greedy and small minded to create wealth through their endeavors. Everything in life has a price of admission, and so do joint ventures. Joint ventures are based on giving, sharing of resources, and creating larger value for everyone involved.

When I form a joint venture, I focus on what I give, not what I get. The more I give away, the richer I get, the happier my investors are to work with me, and the more money I have to invest. The game is simple and easy if you know the rules; the game is impossible if you try to be greedy. The problem with most novice entrepreneurs and investors is that they are conditioned to consume instead of create. We are conditioned to focus on what we are getting, not on what we are giving. Too often we want to own everything entirely by ourselves. So many investors and entrepreneurs are happier to own a single grape than share half of a watermelon.

To pursue the fastest way to real estate wealth, we must kill the greedy person on the inside and focus on creating greater value for our partners, our families, and ourselves.

WHY WE NEED ENTREPRENEURS MORE THAN EVER BEFORE

We are facing a crisis in the US today, and although I am a born Canadian and explicitly not an American, I am concerned for America. America was once the greatest country in the world, an industrial juggernaut and the envy of other nations. America had the best of everything—the best jobs, the best houses, the best companies—and the American dream was desired all over the globe. Immigrants from around the world would risk their lives and the lives of their families to move to America and chase the dream of "making it" in the best country in the world. Today, families who move from Mexico to pursue the American dream are moving back to Mexico because America's dream is over.

The world faces a huge problem while we watch America fall apart. America is supposed to be the poster child of capitalism, a supporter of small and large business, and a place where anyone can make the dream happen. Unfortunately, America is sick because it has more problems than it has entrepreneurs to solve them. Today high schools and universities are churning out record numbers of robotic young people who are programmed to be employees. The sad thing is that these young people have nowhere to go after they step off the conveyor belt of the education system. America does not have enough jobs for these young people, and the trend is becoming global. In China, young men are finishing university decorated with bachelor's, master's, and doctoral degrees with nowhere to go. These people, both American and Chinese, are educated, conditioned, and programmed to look for jobs—not create jobs.

TIMES ARE CHANGING

Current thought leaders would argue that we are entering a new age. Some say the Information Age is over and we are entering the Conceptual

Age. It is no longer good enough to "go to school, get a good job, and save money for retirement." It's time for everyone to become an entrepreneur, at least part time. A career is not enough anymore. In the near future, everyone with a career will also need a side business and a portfolio of investment real estate to maintain a healthy standard of living. The middle class is becoming an endangered species, and job security is disappearing. The average Generation Y or echo boomer will change career paths every four years. Specific career-path skills are less important today than ever; what is more important in the Conceptual Age is to become a generalist, understand general concepts, and be able to put the pieces together. In the Conceptual Age, the creative people, the conceptual people, and the entrepreneurs are becoming the leaders in society. People who can put Money, People, and Deals together will enjoy the greatest freedom in the Conceptual Age, while people who cling to job security, entitlement, and old ideas will have the hardest time of all.

WHO THIS BOOK IS FOR

The Five Million Dollar Book is for those who want to become leaders in the Conceptual Age. It's a book for people who want to create jobs instead of looking for jobs. This book is for people who want to retire early and retire rich. It's a book for people who want more freedom of time and place. This book is for people who want to pursue the shortest way to wealth. This book is for parents who want to look after their children and children who want to look after their parents. This book is for people who embrace change. But most of all, this book is for you.

HOW TO READ THIS BOOK

The Five Million Dollar Book is written in three parts. Part 1 is "The Rules of the Game," and it outlines how the game of Money, People, Deal is played. The first part of this book outlines broad concepts, ideas that must be understood, and rules that must be known to play the game to win.

Part 2, "The Dealmaker, the Mind-Set, and Who You Have to Become," focuses on the mind-set you must develop and the person who you must become in order to be a dealmaker. This section is mostly conceptual and focuses on attitude, because entrepreneurship is 99 percent mind-set. In life, success is built on attitude, not aptitude.

Part 3 is called "The Execution: The Art of Deal" and focuses on components of real estate and making a profit. This section is specific to real estate and offers some unique strategies and techniques to consider when putting together great deals.

At the conclusion of most chapters, you will discover an action step relating to the concepts presented. To get maximum benefit from *The Five Million Dollar Book,* ensure that you follow every action step. You may want to read this book with a notepad and pen to write down your thoughts as you move through the material.

Part 1

THE RULES
OF THE GAME

To win the game, you must first know the rules.
If you don't know the rules, the game is impossible to win.

This section shows you how to play the game
of Money, People, Deal.
I outline broad concepts, ideas that must be understood, and rules
that must be known to play the game to win.

Chapter 1

THE FOUR FASTEST
WAYS TO PROFIT

At any crossroads in life, there are always two paths: the common road and the road less travelled. When it comes to money, most people take the slow way by going to school, getting a good job, and saving for retirement. Like most people, I travelled on the slow road. I went to a good school and graduated with a degree, but my path had a twist on it. After finishing school, although I had earned a degree, I didn't have a set career path or an easy way to success. After I finished school with a major in English and a minor in music, my first job out of school was a ten-dollar-per-hour sales job on straight commission in the middle of the night. I was selling luxury hotel rooms over the telephone and knew the path I was on was not where I wanted to be. I had to learn how to change directions and head down a new avenue. Making ten dollars per hour in the middle of the night was not going to help me live my dreams, and the cold reality of that first job out of university was that I was making more money working part time to pay my way through school than I was earning post education with a degree. In some ways, I may have wasted four years of my life earning that piece of paper that I thought would validate me, but I had also accidentally enrolled in the best school in the world—the school of life.

The blessing in disguise and the lesson I learned very early in life, at age twenty-two, was that there is no set path to success. For myself, I had no illusions. There was no meal ticket; no safe, secure job to cling to; no golden handcuffs to hold me down; no job security to worry about. I had to become an entrepreneur and carve a niche for myself or crawl back into school for more education. Further education was not an option, because I believed the words of Einstein: "Insanity is doing the same thing over and over again and expecting a different result." Instead, I began to study money, business, and entrepreneurship in the school of life, and I learned the most important concept to create all of the wealth I would ever need: Money, People, Deal.

Henry Ford, one of the greatest entrepreneurs of all time, was once asked, "So what, you're a billionaire! What would you do if you lost it all tomorrow?" Mr. Ford replied, "I would have it all back in five years . . . and more!" Donald Trump, one of the most famous real estate investors of our generation, was nearly nine billion dollars in the hole, and he came back richer than ever. Steve Jobs, arguably the best entrepreneur of all time, was kicked out of Apple, the company he founded, only to start a succession of very successful tech companies and return to Apple to make it the most valuable company in history.

What did Henry Ford, Donald Trump, and Steve Jobs all understand that the average person does not? When I began studying business and money, I used to wonder what separated these men, with their ability to create wealth and value out of thin air, from others. What is amazing about all of these men is not just the size of the wealth they have created, but the speed at which they have done so. Henry Ford created all of his wealth in his lifetime and Steve Jobs did the same. Trump had a small head start, but the speed and magnitude of his wealth is just as unexpected.

When I began to study these men, I learned that they all understood how to create wealth by putting Money, People, and Deals together. This is the skill of the entrepreneur and the key to creating the fastest wealth possible. In my business I made the decision to focus on the fastest ways to wealth and placed less emphasis on the slow ways. Life is too short to only rely on the slow ways to reach your destination.

WHY SPEED WINS

In the days of the Roman Empire, war and business were synonymous. War was business and business was war. The entire Roman Empire was built on conquest and plunder. Ancient Romans often became wealthy through the spoils of war and later in life would venture into real estate, trade, or politics. In a similar way, *The Art of War* by Sun Tzu, a brilliant ancient Chinese military strategist, is found in the "business" section of the bookstore instead of the war section. Today, the same principles that apply in warfare also apply in business.

A wise man once said, "Wars are won by legs, not by arms." In history, smaller armies have been able to wear down massive opponents and take victory over large distances: Attila the Hun was able to wreak havoc on the much larger Roman legions by having a small, fast, elite, and mobile force. Erwin Rommel and his Afrika Korps were able to beat the British into the submission in World War II with a small elite, mobile force. Lawrence of Arabia deployed similar tactics in the pre-Second-World-War era that evolved into modern-day guerrilla warfare.

There are two commonalities between Attila the Hun, Erwin Rommel, and Lawrence of Arabia. All three men employed the following into their strategies and tactics: 1) speed and 2) distance.

History has proven that speed and distance are just as powerful on the battlefield as they are in the boardroom. Allow me to show you why.

In business, speed wins. Advantageous terms like "first-mover advantage," "speed of implementation," and "velocity of money" are all concepts that revolve around speed. In business, if you have a chance to be fast or slow, it's usually better to be fast.

In business and warfare, distance is just as important as speed. Strategically, we need to have a short position, a medium position, and a long position, whether we are building a company or managing an investment port-folio. In addition, our lasting power, or "ability to win over distances," whether short, medium, or long, is imperative to success.

Strategies that are effective in short positions may not be effective in me-dium positions, and medium positions will not offer the same advantages as long positions. In business, we need to have an effective mix of three types of strategies to be effective over distances and become leaders in the market.

In my past businesses, I focused too much on long positions and neglected my short and medium positions. I would load up my real estate portfolio with long position buy-and-hold, cash-flowing real estate. In my music business that I ran in university, I poured my time, effort, and energy into producing a long-term brand strategy and forgot my short-term strategy. In my debt-buying business that I started in my early twenties, again, I had a long-term cash flow strategy but no short or medium position.

These cash-poor businesses were aggravating, painful, and hard to grow because there were no short or medium strategies to generate the cash needed to properly grow and expand.

In my early twenties, I spent most of my time working on cash-poor businesses with long-term strategies until I met J. T. Foxx (jtfoxblog.com). J. T. is a successful real estate investor who has transacted hundreds of deals, partnered with some very large money partners, and currently owns a huge speaking and coaching business. When I began to study J. T. and his success, I noticed he weighted his businesses around short positions and the fastest ways to make money.

THE FOUR FASTEST WAYS TO PROFIT

1) **Flipping Real Estate:** Flipping real estate has always been one of the fastest ways to make money in history. Real estate allows an investor to make huge gains with little or no work, and if you do your homework, real estate can be turned in thirty to ninety days with ease. If you're in real estate, flipping should be a strategy used often as part of your portfolio's cash generation strategy. The reason why flipping real estate is so lucrative is because for every dollar you invest, the bank will give you five to ten times what you put in. Instead of making a 5 percent gain, you can make a 50 percent gain in the same amount of time.

2) **Local Marketing/Branding for Other People:** Marketing and branding pre-existing local businesses is a very fast way to make large profits.

Most business people have no clue about marketing and branding, and the market is littered with businesses that are undeveloped and have virtually no marketing. One fast cash-generation strategy is to find a very poorly marketed business or product and rebrand or remarket it. The entire business is pre-existing, so there is essentially very little work to do as far as business building. Selling branding/marketing services is also an extremely fast and lucrative way to make cash.

3) **Public Speaking:** Donald Trump charges $250,000 an hour to speak in public. Other speakers like Raymond Aaron and Tony Robbins, have both made over $1 million an hour giving speeches. Most people would rather be dead than speak in front of an audience. However, this is one of the fastest, most lucrative endeavors for an individual if executed properly. There is enormous leverage in public speaking and tons of opportunity to build a brand. Consider the value of this avenue for a short-term strategy in your business. This strategy can be offered for free (capitalize on branding and lead generation), or it can be monetized for fast profit—who doesn't love options? Why spend an hour selling face-to-face with one prospect when you can fill a room with prospects and sell to one hundred or one thousand prospects at the same time? The leverage in public speaking is tremendous; the profits are enormous, and the speed is unrivaled.

4) **Joint Ventures:** In one year I was able to build up enough residual income to stop working as an employee because I used joint ventures to build my business. Joint ventures are the fastest, highest-leverage business tool available and can be used to build wealth quickly. Only 2 percent of entrepreneurs know how to use joint ventures, and this gives savvy entrepreneurs an enormous advantage. Credit card companies and Fortune 500 companies derive major profits from joint ventures, while small entrepreneurs and investors use zero joint ventures in their business. Whenever I am missing a resource, I will find a joint-venture (JV) partner who has what I am missing. Why try to own everything? I have become a specialist in joint ventures, and I am never low on resources because I know how to create favorable deals for everyone. Some greedy entrepreneurs don't like joint ventures, because they have to give up a percentage of their business for access to extra resources. American billionaire Mark Cuban (blogmaverick.com) frequently asks budding entre-

preneurs on the hit TV show *Shark Tank*, "Would you rather have half a watermelon or a whole grape?" Every time I have to choose between the watermelon and the grape, I choose the watermelon.

After studying the four fastest ways to profit, I began to rethink and re-structure my business. I began to change my business to create balance and generate steady streams of cash. Today my business is healthier than ever, and my strategy going forward has liquidity and an abundance of options.

WHY JOINT VENTURES ARE THE FASTEST WAY TO REAL ESTATE WEALTH

Joint ventures are the fastest way to real estate wealth because no matter what type of resources you start out with, you can make fast profits with real estate joint ventures.

If you have money, but no team of people and no deal, real estate joint ventures are beneficial because you can partner with a successful entre-preneur who has the right skills, knowledge, team, and a profitable deal.

If you have skills, but have no money, you can raise capital if you have a good team of people and a great deal. Money is unlimited for entrepre-neurs who have great deals and good teams of people.

If you have no money and no skills, you can still get wealthy by intro-ducing people with money to smart and savvy real estate entrepreneurs who are looking for money partners. Make sure that you are offered a percentage of the deal for making the introduction, and some entrepre-neurs will even make you an equity partner for making an introduction. In my experience it is always advantageous to pay anyone and everyone for a worthwhile introduction.

WHY I FOCUS ON REAL ESTATE AND JOINT VENTURES

This book, *The Five Million Dollar Book*, focuses on the two fastest ways to real estate wealth: joint ventures and flipping real estate. While I still make use of public speaking and local marketing, I have chosen to gear my entire business around joint ventures and real estate because of the abundance of real estate (it, too, is everywhere) and the abundance of money that is looking for Joint Ventures (it's literally everywhere). I believe in abundance and not scarcity, and that is why I've chosen to run my business with two limitless resources—real estate and joint venture money. Life is too short to take the slow route to wealth; create cash now, learn the rules of the game, and enjoy the fastest way to real estate wealth.

Action Plan: Review the four shortest ways to profit and plan to implement at least one of the four strategies into your business in the next sixty days.

Exclusive Bonus: Go to MoneyPeopleDeal.com and download the Bonus E-Book *Double Your Income with Sandwiches and Postcards.* The password to access your Bonus is "insiderbonus."

Chapter 2

MONEY, PEOPLE, DEAL: THE FASTEST WAY TO REAL ESTATE WEALTH

I am often amazed at how lazy new investors can be with their money. Often a novice real estate investor is someone in their thirties or forties, tired of their job, and making a steady median income. Since they have a stable job, this person is able to obtain easy credit and financing from banks. Often these investors will have access to a home equity line of credit, a wide arsenal of credit cards, and will have an RRSP account (the Canadian equivalent of an American 401(k) account) with $30,000 to $40,000 (if they're responsible), and have $10,000 to $20,000 cash savings ready to do a deal. These investors are tired of the rat race and are ready to take the plunge into real estate with their own money.

The sad thing is that this type of new investor has been working since they were eighteen to reach this cash position, and they are now in their midthirties and ready to start investing. This investor has done things the slow way, and it has cost them decades of their life to reach this position. Time is the only real currency in life, and to do things faster, we must be educated. Education is where all wealth comes from because all wealth originates in the mind.

No matter how prepared we are or how much money we start with, the truth of the matter is, in business or real estate, we will always run out of money. No matter how much cash and credit we have, it always gets 'tied up' in a deal, and we eventually run out. This happens to every investor, whether you are Donald Trump or Warren Buffett. There is always a point where the investor must go out and raise capital to keep investing.

I began investing at age twenty-two, and the greatest advantage I acquired by starting so young is that I had virtually no cash, no credit, and no credibility when I started. I had to learn to raise cash, manage my small amount of credit, and leverage credibility. I had to learn the skills required to play the game of Money, People, Deal with no cash from day one because I started the game with nothing. I was a punk kid who had taken $2,000 worth of real estate seminars and had to make the dream happen.

My investing career didn't take off until I learned the rules for creating deals and raising money. This skill set has allowed me to raise money for all of my deals (except my first one, where I put down a small down payment of $1,200 cash). Because I understand the fundamentals of Money, People, Deal, I have never put down money on an acquisition of business or real estate since.

Most investors think that cash is king, and they are terrified of raising money for a deal. The truth is that cash is trash; everyone has it, and it's a cheap commodity that is worthless without the brains to manage it. Money is fickle and is easily attracted if we understand a few key principles of money.

There are three major parts to putting a deal together and raising all the cash we will ever need. They are the following:

1) The Money: The cash required to start the business or acquire the real estate.

2) The People: The *team* that will operate the business or asset.

3) The Deal: The business or asset itself.

The Three Major Parts of Putting a Deal Together

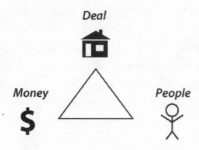

Fig 1.0

Most novice investors don't understand the three fundamental parts of a real estate deal and waste time trying to raise money the wrong way. By doing so, they burn their credibility and look like fools to their network of potential investors.

WHAT ARE THE THREE THINGS REQUIRED TO START A BUSINESS IN ANY INDUSTRY?

Whenever I ask this question to a group of people, the first answer is usually "Money!" and this answer is 100 percent correct. Money is always required, in some shape or form, to start a business, whether it is $10 to start a lemonade stand or $10 million to build an apartment complex. When I say that I started my business with no money, what this means is that I started my business with someone else's money. The money used to acquire real estate was raised from an investor and has grown by leaps and bounds with other people's money. Money alone is useless and earns very low returns without the other parts of the business. Money is abundant; everyone has it, and money is always looking for a safe place to earn a handsome return.

The second ingredient required to start any business is the people who form the team that will run and operate the business. They often represent the management and the technical knowledge of the business.

The third ingredient required to start a business is the deal. Deals can be real estate properties, traditional businesses, patented gadgets, Internet businesses, etc. For the purpose of this book, we will focus on real estate as the deal, but keep in mind that a deal can be any business that makes money. In many ways, a good deal is the most valuable part of the business, especially if it's proprietary or hard to find. A good deal can be like a magnet, quickly attracting the people and the money to get the deal done. In contrast, a bad deal can be impossible to fund.

Money, People, Deal is the game of entrepreneurship, and it has the highest rewards out of any game for those who know how to play. An entrepreneur who can assemble Money, People, and Deals will enjoy the highest returns possible while making his investors rich.

MONEY, PEOPLE, DEAL— RULES OF THE GAME

1) The rules are simple: those who can obtain two of the three pieces required to assemble a business will get the third. For example, if you have the Deal and the People, the Money will come every time. I have never had a deal fall apart because of lack of funding.

Rules of the Game

Point 1: "If you have 2 pieces of the puzzle, the third will come."

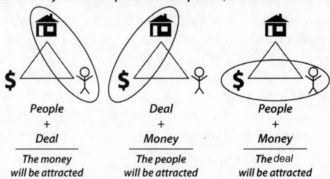

People	Deal	People
+	+	+
Deal	Money	Money
The money will be attracted	*The people will be attracted*	*The deal will be attracted*

Fig 1.1

2) If you only have control of one of the three pieces, you have nothing. In the game, you are worth nothing if you can't make a transaction happen.

  a) If you only have money, you are a bank, a funding source, an angel investor, or a lender.

  b) If you only have people, you are a contractor.

  c) If you only have a deal, you are a bird dog or a wholesaler.

  d) If you can put all three together, you are an entrepreneur and will reap the highest rewards.

Rules of the Game

Point 2: "If you only have one piece, you have nothing."

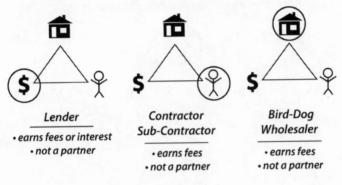

<table>
<tr><td align="center">**Lender**</td><td align="center">**Contractor
Sub-Contractor**</td><td align="center">**Bird-Dog
Wholesaler**</td></tr>
<tr><td align="center">• earns fees or interest
• not a partner</td><td align="center">• earns fees
• not a partner</td><td align="center">• earns fees
• not a partner</td></tr>
</table>

Fig 1.2

3) The most valuable piece in the game is the Deal. The better the deal, the easier it is to find the money. If you are incompetent or don't want to do the Deal, you can always sell to another investor for a fee. Selling deals as a wholesaler or a bird dog can be very lucrative, and I recommend it every day of the week. The money you can make selling deals is fantastic when measured against your effort.

4) The least valuable piece in the game is the Money. This is because everyone has access to it. Money earns virtually nothing on its own and gets robbed by inflation. Since money is constantly depreciating, it must move to be valuable. Money can come from literally any source

for almost any price. Cash investors will line up for a good deal and will compete for a great deal if they know it's a winner.

5) People are interchangeable and so is the entrepreneur running the business. Entrepreneurs are part of the people team and must build a good team and management style to run the business effectively. Entrepreneurs who develop a brand over time can become nearly impossible to replace.

6) The deal drives the whole game and is the king of the three pieces. The deal is the piece you should seek first (in my opinion). You can always sell it to another investor if you can't pull it off. I love buying deals from investors who want to pass or cannot close.

Novice Investors
"Try to raise money without a deal or team."

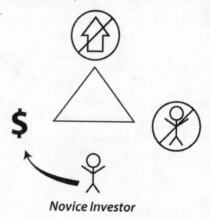

Novice Investor

Fig 1.3

Too many novice investors try to raise money without a team or a proper deal. In my opinion, this is absolutely the wrong approach.

The easiest way to play the game of Money, People, Deal is to:

1) Find a deal first, get it under contract with an escape clause, and allow yourself a due diligence period (or another condition) to delay your contract.

2) While the deal is tied up, begin assembling the team required to execute the deal.

The Easiest Way To Play:

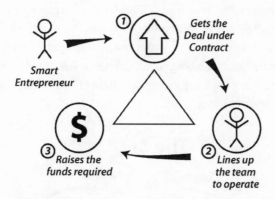

Fig 1.4

3) Once you have the deal under control and the people under control, begin shopping investors for money. Always have a professional business plan/loan proposal prepared.

Show your investors:

1. The best-case scenario—In this scenario, the deal performs better than anticipated; everyone wins, and everyone is happy.

2. The realistic case scenario—In this scenario, the deal performs as expected, slightly better or slightly worse. This is generally what investors expect.

3. The worst-case scenario—The deal performs worse than expected. In this scenario, there generally are no profits and the investors are lucky to recover their cash.

4. The *nightmare* scenario—The deal becomes illiquid; it cannot be sold for nearly the value that you have invested. The investors will have to wait to get their money out or sell at a loss. This is even worse than the worst-case scenario.

It's important to show your investors these scenarios and make sure they're OK with losing all of their money or recovering from a nightmare scenario.

Once you have two different investors interested in funding you, you have enough interest to negotiate and get one investor to commit. I like to split all of my deals fifty-fifty with my money partners because I don't like to haggle and "bite the hand that feeds." I prefer to overpay and reward my partners for investing in me. When I call my investors in the future, they will be delighted to do more deals with me and have a check ready for me within twenty-four hours. I have proven I can make a profit for my repeat deal partners, and they are happy to get a call from me because they know they're going to make money.

The Split

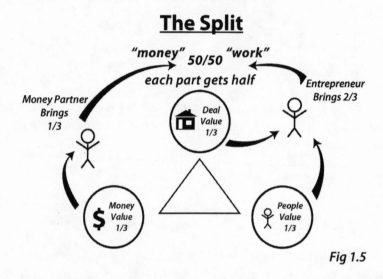

Fig 1.5

WHY DOES "THE MONEY" LOVE THE MONEY, PEOPLE, DEAL PROCESS?

Although "The Money" only accounts for one third of the resources, they get to take half of the deal. Where in life can you bring one third of the resources and walk away with half? The answer is marriage. Many marriage partners come together with unequal resources, yet if there is a split of resources through a divorce, each party gets half. I like to overpay my money partners and give them half of the deal to create loyalty and excitement.

AFTER YOUR FIRST RAISE, BEGIN BUILDING A TRACK RECORD, DOCUMENT EVERY DEAL INTO A TRACK RECORD, THEN RINSE AND REPEAT!

You can repeat the Money, People, Deal process an unlimited number of times, and you will never run out of capital. By using this process, you will be tapping into the infinite amount of cash that is looking for profitable deals every day. Eventually, you will have more money waiting in your pipeline than deals, and then you will want to find people to bring you deals to keep your machine running. This is a great position to be in, and one that I frequently enjoy. This means the time has come to expand into a greater volume of deals or into larger opportunities.

Raising money is the ultimate skill of the entrepreneur and one that everyone should learn to perfect. I learned this skill early in life, and it has fueled my success so far. As long as I continue to create profit for my investors, capital will always be available for me. "Give a man a fish and he's fed for a day, teach a man to fish and he's fed for life."

Action Step: Think about the last time you attempted to raise money and ask yourself: *Which of the three pieces did I have before raising capital? Was I prepared with an adequate business plan? Was I successful or unsuccessful? What went wrong, and what could have gone smoother?*

Chapter 3

MONEY DOES NOT EQUAL WEALTH

The English language can play tricks on those who don't spend the time to learn its nuances. Many people think that retirement accounts and mutual funds are the same; cash and credit are the same; and money and wealth are the same.

RETIREMENT ACCOUNTS (A.K.A RRSPS IN CANADA OR 401(K)S IN THE US) AND MUTUAL FUNDS ARE NOT THE SAME.

When I used to work in the investment industry, I would be absolutely stunned by the amount of people who could not differentiate between their RRSP retirement account and their mutual funds. For most people, their retirement accounts have only ever held mutual funds, only hold mutual funds today, and only will hold mutual funds in the future. For these people, the terms *mutual fund* and *RRSP account* might as well be the same. However, RRSPs and mutual funds are not the same at all.

IF A SHOEBOX WERE AN RRSP ACCOUNT, MUTUAL FUNDS WOULD BE A PAIR OF SHOES INSIDE THE BOX.

An investor can put any pair of shoes they wish inside the box, and it's still an RRSP account. If mutual funds are brown shoes, the brown shoes can be taken out of the box and replaced with a pair of black shoes, which could represent a privately held mortgage. Many savvy investors with RRSP accounts use their RRSPs to buy investment real estate instead of mutual funds.

Shoes and Shoeboxes

You can invest in real estate with your RRSP account

Mutual
Funds

Privately Held Mortgage for
Investing in Real Estate

"brown shoes" RRSP   "black shoes" RRSP

Fig 1.6

CASH AND CREDIT ARE NOT THE SAME.

Many Canadians have seen windfall equity gains on their homes in the last ten years. The rush of doubling or tripling the value of the family home has made many Canadians feel rich. Of course, when we feel rich, we start to act rich, and suddenly we are using our newly gained home equity to purchase vacations to Mexico, a new car, or renovate the kitchen. What many Canadians don't realize is that equity spent on consumer goods like vacations, cars, or home improvements creates bad debt. Like all debt, home equity needs to be paid back with interest at some point. The equity in the home is not cash; it's debt, but many people spend like they have won the lottery.

Although home equity is not cash, it can be treated like cash and be used to purchase cash-flowing investment property or to flip real estate for profit. The lines today between cash and credit are blurrier than ever. With credit being offered at record lows, cheap interest rates, cash, and credit in many ways have become the same. When interest rates go back up to their historic levels, cash and credit will look very different again.

MONEY AND WEALTH ARE NOT THE SAME.

Money and wealth are two words that are easy to confuse. Most people use money and wealth interchangeably and say, *My uncle has money* or *My uncle is wealthy.* The meanings on the surface appear to be the same, but money and wealth are vastly different.

WEALTH IS MEASURED IN TIME; MONEY IS MEASURED IN DOLLARS.

The biggest distinction between wealth and money lies in the units of measurement. Wealth is measured in time, and money is measured in dollars. For example, if you are living paycheck to paycheck, you only have two weeks' worth of wealth. If you stopped working, you could only survive for two weeks. If you owned a large real estate portfolio that provided you with more passive income than you need to live, then you can say that you are infinitely wealthy because you can survive forever without working again.

WHY WILL A NEST EGG MENTALITY WILL LEAVE YOU BROKE?

Money is much easier to understand than the intangible concept of wealth. Many people in the world have money but have zero wealth. One example I can think of is the traditional Canadian retiree. Traditional investment advisors preach that you need a "nest egg" for retirement. These advisors will say that the average Canadian needs one million, two million, or three million dollars to live off of during retirement. The sad thing is that the investment advisor is planning for their client to sit on two million dollars of cash and slowly eat away at the nest egg. If the nest egg runs out, so does the ability to survive. Many investment advisors today are setting their clients up to have money in retirement, but absolutely no wealth. To me this is scary, because we cannot estimate what the cost of living will be in the future. What will the cost of living be five, ten, or fifteen years from now? I don't have a crystal ball, but I know that it will be higher than today.

WILL TWO MILLION DOLLARS BE ENOUGH?

I was recently reading a column in the *Globe and Mail* in which a traditional investment advisor offers weekly advice for a particular Canadian's investment portfolio. The advisor was evaluating the portfolio of a fifty-five-year-old Toronto woman with a positive net worth of two million dollars. The advisor's message to the woman was, "You cannot afford to retire." Although this woman had two million dollars in assets, including her home, he advised that she continue to work, because two million dollars was no longer enough to retire in Toronto. The woman in the newspaper column is someone with money, but no wealth. In the 1970s, two million dollars was a lot of money; in today's dollars two million dollars may not be enough to retire on.

WE NEED WEALTH MORE THAN EVER BEFORE—AND HERE'S WHY.

Most people wake up in the morning, have a shower, get dressed, and go to work to earn money. The problem is that most of us are not working to build wealth. Wealth is passive income that comes in every month whether we work or not. We need wealth more than ever before because the world is changing at a record pace. We no longer know what industries, businesses, and jobs will be relevant five years from now. In 2005 Myspace.com ruled the Internet and was sold for billions of dollars. By 2013, Myspace.com became a dinosaur with virtually no relevance on the Internet. We need to have a strong base of real estate wealth because, unlike high-tech companies like Myspace.com, real estate is a primitive, slow, and stable way to build real wealth.

Action Step: Evaluate your current financial situation. Do you have money, wealth, or neither? What resources do you have at your disposal to build wealth? Do you have an underutilized RRSP or 401(k) retirement account or home equity line of credit? How much monthly passive income do you need to achieve wealth and stop working?

Chapter 4

THE SKILLS REQUIRED TO PLAY THE GAME.

Although Money, People, Deal is one of the most rewarding games in the world, it is certainly not the easiest game to play. To effectively raise money for real estate, an entrepreneur must be proficient in all seven of the following skill sets:

1) Sales and Marketing
2) People Skills
3) Management Skills
4) Deal-Finding Skills
5) Deal-Analyzing Skills
6) Negotiation Skills
7) Closing Skills

Everyone has a strength, and everyone has a weakness; no one is perfect in all seven skill sets required for the game. As for myself, I am proficient at sales and marketing, deal finding, and negotiating. My weakness out of the seven skill sets would be management. There is nothing wrong with identifying your strengths and weaknesses; in fact, knowing where you excel and where you are weak is extremely powerful. Everyone is different, and depending on how your brain is naturally wired, you will be strong and weak in different areas.

Action Step: Examine the following seven skill sets and give yourself a score from one to ten, with ten being the strongest and one being the weakest in each category. This exercise will give you some insight into which skills need to be delegated to a partner, contractor, or employee, and which skills can be performed best by you.

1) **Sales and Marketing** (score 1 to 10)—This is the primary skill for raising money for real estate deals and the skill that is most important in the game of Money, People, Deal. Consider the following:

   a. Do you have formal full-time sales experience?
   b. Do you enjoy making cold calls?
   c. Do you have a sales script and sales process?
   d. Do you enjoy selling?
   e. Are you a natural sales person?
   f. Do you enjoy presenting?
   g. Do you enjoy promoting and marketing?

2) **People Skills** (score 1 to 10)—People skills are important in real estate. Real estate, like every business, is a people business, and every single part of the business requires some form of interaction with people.

   a. Does working with people energize you?
   b. Are you a good listener when conversing with others?
   c. Can you relate to other people?
   d. Do you have leadership skills to lead a team?
   e. Do you have a pleasant personality?
   f. Can you spot talented people and avoid troublesome people?
   g. Can you handle conflict and communicate effectively?

3) **Management Skills** (score 1 to 10)—Management skills are important for running the business of real estate.

   a. Are you able to organize information effectively and access it in the future?
   b. Are you able to create and follow processes?
   c. Do you keep an organized and well-run back office?
   d. Do you follow up effectively with team members to ensure that tasks are getting done?
   e. Are you effective at correcting ineffective processes and team members?

f. Are you effective at motivating and leading teams of people?

g. Do you command respect from your team members?

4) **Deal-Finding Skills** (score 1 to 10)—Deal-finding skills are very important to the game of Money, People, Deal. Deals drive the whole business, and the ability to find a great deal is an extremely important skill.

a. Can you quickly and effectively find distressed property on the MLS service?

b. Do you work well with Realtors® to find deals with equity in them?

c. Are you familiar with multiple markets and submarkets to find desirable areas?

d. Can you spot mismarketed and mismanaged properties and see the opportunity?

e. Do you know which properties are profit killers and which to avoid?

f. Do you run ad campaigns to target distressed sellers?

g. Do you have a network of lawyers, property managers, and other investors who can send you deals?

5) **Deal-Analyzing Skills** (score 1 to 10)—Being able to find a great deal is one thing; being able to analyze a deal for profit is another skill all together.

a. Do you have access to multiple strategies to evaluate a property from different angles?

b. Are you familiar with sold prices per square foot in select markets in your area?

c. Are you familiar with rent rates in your area?

d. Do you have strategies to increase the profitability of a given property?

e. Can you create an accurate pro forma for a best case, realistic case, worst case, and nightmare case scenario?

f. Do your numbers have padding and reserve accounts built in?

6) **Negotiation Skills** (score 1 to 10)—Great negotiation skills can make the difference between an average deal and a spectacular deal. Negotiating is the key to getting a no-money-down deal, equity on day

one, or excellent terms.

    a. When negotiating, do you focus on a win-win scenario or a win-lose scenario?

    b. Do you learn the motivation of the vendor when negotiating?

    c. Are you able to properly present a terms deal and get it accepted?

    d. Do you formally study negotiating and recognize it as a skill that requires constant improvement?

    e. When negotiating, do you "give and take" as circumstances change? Do you offer strategic trades to get what you want?

7) **Closing Skills** (score 1 to 10)—Closing is a skill that can make the difference between a profitable deal done and no deal done.

    a. Do you operate with short, written-down deadlines?

    b. Do have a hard or soft closing style?

    c. Do you always make a point of asking for the business?

    d. Do you follow up with team members to ensure they're finishing important tasks?

    e. How do you handle objections? Are you able to create win-win scenarios for everyone?

Action Step: After you have evaluated the seven skill sets required to play Money, People, Deal, organize the skill sets from strongest (scores closest to ten) to weakest (scores closest to one) and determine your strengths and weaknesses. Your top three strengths should be your greatest skills that you bring to your team and your three weaknesses should be the skills that you delegate to other team members. Remember, no one is perfect, and we can't be excellent at all seven skill sets—it's impossible. Focus on your strengths and delegate in the area of your weaknesses to run your business efficiently.

Chapter 5

RISK TOLERANCE: HOW DO YOU PERSONALLY DEFINE RISK?

In life, there is no such thing as a guarantee. Everything we do always has an element of risk, even everyday actions like driving to work or crossing the street.

I googled the definition of risk, and this definition came up from thefree-dictionary.com:

risk (rsk)

n.

1. The possibility of suffering harm or loss; danger.

2. A factor, thing, element, or course involving uncertain danger; a hazard: *"the usual risks of the desert: rattlesnakes, the heat, and lack of water"* *(Frank Clancy).*

3.
a. The danger or probability of loss to an insurer.
b. The amount that an insurance company stands to lose.

4.

a. The variability of returns from an investment.

b. The chance of nonpayment of a debt.

All of the definitions above involve some form of loss, hazard, suffering, and an element of variability, probability, or chance. What I find intriguing about risk is that every single person I meet has a different subjective definition. Often, when I am discussing risk with another investor, I will ask what their personal definition of risk is. More often than not, investors will define risk as the chance or probability that they lose on an investment. This common definition is sufficient, but I find it to be an unsophisticated definition because it does not address control.

Robert Kiyosaki, author of the *Rich Dad Poor Dad* series of books, says that intelligence is the ability to make distinctions. The more distinctions we can make, the more intelligent we are. For example, there are over 7,500 variations of apples in the world. When it comes to apples, I am unintelligent and can only name a few variations: Red Delicious, Granny Smith, crab apples, and Macintosh. A person who can name one hundred variations of apples is much more intelligent than I am on the subject of apples. When I hear a person's definition of risk, I can immediately find out what their sophistication level is when it comes to business and investing.

My personal definition of risk has changed many times throughout my life. I used to believe in luck, and now I do not. All I believe in is actions performed and numbers. Life and business are a numbers game; if you can produce the volume and hit the numbers, you will succeed every time. There is no luck.

My definition of risk is an inventory of the elements that are under your control compared with an inventory of elements that are out of your control.

Ask yourself, *Am I comfortable with my degree of control?* If you are comfortable, then you may proceed with the risk. If you are not comfortable with the degree of control, then do not proceed.

My definition of risk has two primary distinctions that the average definition does not:

1) My definition of risk assesses your degree of control in a situation.

2) My definition of risk assesses your emotions and how you feel about your level of control.

Notice that I eliminate "probability" or "chance" from my definition of risk. In my world, actions and options are more important than probability. No matter how bad a scenario gets, there are always actions to be performed and options that can be explored. Probability and chance come from past data, and may or may not apply to the present or the future.

Naturally, there are things that can happen outside of my control, and I must address and mitigate all contingencies before proceeding. Should something outside of my control become an issue, the question is: how do we recover from this position? In my world, I understand that in life and in business, plans fail, people fail, systems fail, and markets fail. And what is more important than relying on all these imperfect elements is to understand how to recover and "fix" the failures. I build failure and multiple contingency plans into my ventures and understand that failure and recovery are part of the game.

In real estate, between 5 percent and 10 percent on the balance sheet of a buy and hold will be factored in for vacancy on multifamily buildings. On a buy, fix, and sell, at least 3 percent will be factored in as a "sales discount," meaning we cannot plan on selling at full price. Restaurants and traditional businesses will build theft into their balance sheets. Sophisticated business people understand that failure, loss, and recovery are all part of the game and factor it in to their projections and balance sheets in advance.

My definition understands that there are elements in our control and out of our control. There is no luck—only degrees of control. If you are OK with your degree of control, then proceed with the risk. Of course, there is always that moment where we must take a "leap of faith," and no amount of due diligence can protect us from the elements out of our control.

What is most important when entering an endeavor with risk is to ask yourself, *How do I escape if I want to exit?* For myself, one of the reasons I love real estate is that no matter how bad the deal goes, there is always a large tangible asset attached to the venture that can be liquidated to recover the investor's capital.

Again, we come back to elements under control and elements out of control. When raising capital from an investor or considering a "risky" venture, take them through the following scenarios to asses if the venture is right for them: the best case, the realistic case, the worst case, and the nightmare case.

As for myself, I have a low risk tolerance, and I always say to my capital partners, "If you are OK with the nightmare scenario, then we are OK to do business."

At the end of the day, risk is all about emotions. If we are emotionally OK with our degree of control and how the nightmare scenario would affect our life, then we are ready for the risk. If you cannot handle the elements that are out of control and would not be able to live with the nightmare scenario, then the risk is not for you. There is a famous saying "Nothing ventured, nothing gained," and we must all take calculated risks in our pursuit of success. The question is, after exploring a few definitions of risk, How do you personally define risk going forward?

Your personal definition of risk is extremely important because it will define which risks to take and which ones to avoid. To paraphrase Sun Tzu, know yourself and know your enemy, and you will be victorious in every battle.

Action Step: Write down three elements that you must be in control of when investing in a real estate deal. Also write down three elements you are comfortable leaving outside of your control.

Chapter 6

INSIDER TRADING AND
WHY YOU NEED TO DO IT

In stocks, insider trading is illegal. In real estate, insider trading is essential.

In any market, there are insiders and there are outsiders. When corporate executives on Wall Street buy or sell stocks in their own companies with "insider knowledge," they go to jail. When a real estate investor gets first chance to purchase a property privately without public knowledge, he can get rich.

Markets like Wall Street are set up like casinos, and TV stations like Canada's BNN (Business News Network) are funded by stockbrokers to create excitement and encourage trading. Stockbrokers get paid when trades happen, so they want their audience on BNN to get emotional and make as many trades as possible. BNN will run stories that pump up the emotions of the audience just to make money; the information is not provided to make actual sound investment decisions.

When emotions go up, intelligence goes down; in a casino, the house always wins. And when it comes to stocks, you are not the house.

In my opinion, the stock market is not designed for the average investor to win. Rather, it's a game played by insiders and institutional investors. For the average retail investor, there is very little control in stocks—unless you're an insider.

I prefer to control my investments, control the management, and control the outcome of my returns. I also prefer to make purchases as an insider with access to the necessary information to make profitable decisions.

Information is king in the market, and those who control the information control the market.

In real estate you become an insider by

1) Belonging to a large network of other investors
2) Maintaining a large network of lawyers
3) Posting private advertisements for deals
4) Offering referral programs
5) Working with a large network of Realtors®
6) Speaking in front of groups of investors or the public
7) Creating content, blogs, and videos for consumption
8) Working with a network of property managers
9) Working with a network of private lenders
10) Becoming the biggest, most visible person in the market

The truth is that becoming an insider is quite simple in real estate. The best deals always come to those who are 1) most visible, 2) most connected, and, 3) most in control of the information in the market.

When a real estate deal hits the local market with a Realtor®, the deal has already been cherry-picked by at least eight sets of eyes. The fewer sets of eyeballs that see the deal before hitting the market, the higher the chances are to profit.

In high school it's easier to date the bookworm girl who is cloistered in the library than it is to date the prom queen. The prom queen has so many more sets of eyeballs on her, so her value is pumped way up and overinflated. There is a lineup of guys dying to get a chance to talk to her because she is visible and well marketed. Avoid the prom queen at all costs and go for the bookworm. With some lipstick and high heels, she can easily be the prom queen, but with much less competition and at a much lower cost.

This analogy applies directly to real estate. By the time a house hits the retail market, multiple Realtors® have looked at it, at least one broker, a few secretaries, a handful of assistants, everyone in the seller's immediate circle, all of the Realtor's® best clients, all of the broker's best clients, their contractors, and then all the other retail buyers who get to it first.

By the time the property gets to you, everyone has explored any easy chances for profit, and you are usually too late to the party. Plus, you now have to pay the price that the seller wanted, plus the commissions of two Realtors® and two brokers. Negotiating becomes muddled because the Realtors® always have their own interests above their clients, and some-times the brokers can complicate negotiations as well.

When all of these "professionals" get involved, prices begin to rise, and favorable terms disappear. All options for good terms or no-money-down deals go out the window because the Realtors® will kill any chances of a "creative deal." They want to get paid their commissions immediately and do not care about the price or terms of the deal: they just want the transaction to happen regardless of whether the buyer or seller gets a favorable deal.

However, when you become an insider, or partner with an insider, you get first access to deals before anyone else gets a chance to look.

The best deals I have done have come from

> 1) Other investors who could not close on private deals
> 2) Private ads I have placed
> 3) My networks and relationships

Being active in the market, participating in local investor groups, having an online presence, private advertising, and public speaking have created an insider position for me in my market. Being visible and sending a clear message that I am "always looking for deals" has attracted excellent opportunities that are well under market value, under appraised value, 100 percent vendor financed, or no money down. The average person believes these deals do not exist or are not possible in their local market. The truth is that these deals are available everywhere, but you need to become an insider or partner with an insider to take advantage of them.

The best deals are made and are not advertised on the market because they never ever make it to market. This rule applies to any market: the best girls to date are not advertised on eHarmony®, PlentyOfFish, or at the local bar. To find real value in life and in the market, we must gain insider access, become well connected and visible, and control the information around us.

The best deals are reserved for insiders; everyone else can pay full price.

Chapter 7

BUY TIME AND TALENT

It always amazes me to see the thought patterns of novice and interme-diate real estate investors. In Winnipeg (my home market) properties are relatively cheap compared to the rest of Canada. Properties are even considered "affordable" when compared to other markets in Canada. Winnipeg scores very well on the national affordability index.

But here's the downside of being so affordable . . .

Since properties are "affordable" in Winnipeg, many novice and inter-mediate real estate investors get lazy and actually use their own cash and lines of credit to buy properties. Eventually, they will always run out of cash or credit, and then they stop growing their portfolios instead of changing their mind-sets. What I see happen in Winnipeg is that we have a good number of investors who have decent day jobs, between one and ten doors (depending on the age of the investor), and their resources are usually tied up or close to maxed out.

To grow the real estate business further, it's time to think outside the box.

I bought my first deal at the age of twenty-three and had no cash from day one. So if I wanted to play the game, I had to operate with no cash. Every dollar that comes into my business is re-invested—but not into properties, because I play the game of no cash.

So where does my money go when I earn it? What do I buy instead of saving up for down payments? How do I operate a real estate business with no cash?

There are two things I think every entrepreneur/real estate investor should be purchasing with their hard-earned dollars—**and it's not more property!**

If you want to grow your business at an exponential and geometric rate, you must buy two things: time and talent.

There is a term in investing and business called "velocity." Velocity is the speed at which money moves. When I started out in real estate investing, I was focused on doing one to two deals a year. I was a very low-velocity investor, and I actually tried to use my own cash and credit (which didn't take me far because I had virtually none).

At the time of this writing, I am considered an intermediate investor (classified by one transaction a month), and I'm heading toward advanced investor (classified by hundreds of transactions a year). The velocity of novice investors, intermediate investors, and advanced investors varies greatly and is the key to moving forward in your career.

What separates "the men from the boys" when considering intermediate vs. advanced investors? In a general sense, there are only two things differentiating the two: time and talent.

In the past, my mentality was to use my resources to save up or raise funds for a slow buy and hold. Today my mentality is to use my resources to create lead generation, websites, brands, videos, blogs, articles, photos, seminars, billboards, employees, teams of bird dogs, databases, referral programs, books, and social media campaigns to build a web of influence. This web grabs large amounts of leads and maximizes the dollars generated per lead.

All of these bells and whistles attract properties, money partners, and strategic partners to me. I have access to the best opportunities and have exponentially increased my chances of success.

To create and maintain this web of influence, I need time and talent. There is no way I can build all of these things with my limited technical knowledge and finite time.

I buy time by outsourcing a lot of my tasks. Digital tasks are outsourced on Elance.com or crowdspring.com. I can leverage my dollars by purchasing time in depressed economies where time and talent can be purchased for pennies on the dollar. Physical tasks are outsourced to local contractors or delegated to strategic partners, who take a share of the profits.

I buy talent in the same way. I make sure to attract the best talent to my teams, pay people what they ask or more, invest in bonus and reward structures, and keep my machine well oiled. Coaches and mentors are a new addition to my payroll this year. Free advice is too expensive for me now. You only get ahead in this business by paying to get ahead, and you get to choose to pay for advancement in blood, sweat, tears, time, or money. You can pay in any way you like, and I've already paid in blood, sweat, and tears. I have also paid for my knowledge with time by volunteering and working for free. Paying to advance my game with money is the most efficient way to move ahead. "An average man learns from his mistakes; a genius learns from other people's mistakes."

Paid coaches are extremely expensive, but the knowledge and foresight I get from spending time with people who have reached the "advanced" level of investing is absolutely priceless. I often see investors scoff at the prices that some coaches and mentors charge, but I think their expertise is worth every penny. Why reinvent the wheel? Just hire someone onto your team who knows how to build the wheel—it's really simple. I know I cannot do everything myself and must purchase time and talent to reach my goal of "advanced investor."

Reaching one's goals isn't easy, but with the right thinking, systems, and coaches, it isn't too hard either. For instance, my goal in 2012 was to do twelve deals. I met that goal fairly easily without a lot of help. In 2013 my plan was then to do one hundred deals. The biggest challenge in making a quantum leap in performance is to think differently than I have in the past. A danger I have moving forward is that I have already achieved a degree of success, but not the level I want. I can guarantee I won't be painting suites or driving around looking at properties every day if I'm going to achieve one hundred deals. Doing everything myself, with my time and resources, is far too inefficient to achieve success. Instead, I will be purchasing massive amounts of time and talent to execute my strategic plans.

Action Step: Are you purchasing time and talent in your business? If you are, are you purchasing enough? What are you missing? Who are you missing? Who do you have to hire to get you to the next level? How do you need to change your thinking?

Chapter 8

PARTNERSHIPS FOR LIFE

Lead generation is easily one of the biggest expenses for any business. It costs nearly seven times more dollars and effort to attract a new client than it does to sell to a pre-existing client. With that being said, why do most businesses, investors, and entrepreneurs focus mostly on trying to find new business than build on their pre-existing client base?

As for myself, when I became a full-time investor, I made the goal of doing twelve deals in my first year. Logically, I figured I would need twelve different investors (one per deal); every month I would have to find one deal and one investor. The math made sense, the logic made sense, but what happened in the field when I began to execute my plans did not make sense.

I did my first deal of the year with a family friend of mine and my second deal with a teacher from my high school. My third deal was with an acquaintance named Mack, whom I did not know that well, but he shared the same passion for investing that I did. I showed Mack a distressed house in downtown Winnipeg, and he told me he was ready to invest. The two of us spent twenty-one days renovating the house every day for at least eight hours a day, seven days a week. We put in a lot of long evenings in the house and became friends while we invested our sweat equity. After the renovations were done, we filled the house with a tenant, and I began looking for my next investor.

What happened next shocked me. I mentioned to Mack that I had a new deal under contract, and he said he wanted it. I figured Mack would do one deal with me and then maybe next year he would consider doing another one; instead, Mack ended up doing my fourth deal with me, and then my fifth deal. Before the year was over, Mack was also doing two flips with me for a total of five deals in the year! Without planning for it or asking for it, Mack quickly became 40 percent of my business; he was a repeat customer, liked what I was doing, trusted me, and wanted to invest more. My initial prediction of needing twelve different investors was completely wrong. By the end of the year, I had done twelve deals with only six investors; repeat business was taking over the new business. By the end of the year, I could not even get a new investor into my business because my pre-existing investors were monopolizing all of my deals.

Later in the year, I began to adopt a "partners-for-life" strategy I learned from J. T. Foxx. J. T. built his business by creating lifelong relationships with his current investors and very quickly had access to all of the capital he would ever need. J. T. used a program called the "Seth Model," named after his first partner Seth, who helped him raise millions of dollars to run his business.

The Seth Model is extremely powerful because it creates a special synergy between the working partner (J. T.) and the money partner (Seth) that allows both of them to grow very large very quickly—even when both partners run out of cash! The truth in real estate is that no matter how much money you start with, you will always run out. Seth started with $250,000 cash, and once they did a few deals with fifty-fifty ownership, Seth was out of money.

SETH MODEL FIRST GENERATION

Seth has $250,000 cash to invest and all profits are split between J. T. and Seth as follows:

50 percent, J. T.
50 percent, Seth

Seth Model

1st generation

Funding Deals

JT 50% | SETH (250k) 50%

Fig 1.7

To bring more money to the partnership, J. T. and Seth worked out an agreement that if Seth brought a larger partner into the fold, Seth would get 10 percent of the second-generation partnership and have no money invested; J. T. would get 50 percent of the partnership and would do all of the work. The new partner would get 40 percent of the second-generation partnership and provide the capital. The new partner got 40 percent of the partnership instead of 50 percent because, at this point, J. T. had a proven track record, rather than the unproven track record that Seth took a 50 percent split on. Seth took a greater risk, so Seth got a greater reward.

SETH MODEL SECOND GENERATION

Seth is out of cash; Seth finds a two-million-dollar partner in his network and makes him a 40 percent partner. The new partner gets 40 percent of the partnership instead of 50 percent because J. T. and Seth have a proven track record.

50 percent, J. T.
10 percent, Seth
40 percent, two-million-dollar partner

Once the second-generation partnership is out of cash, it's up to the largest partner to bring an even larger partner to the third-generation partnership. Where Seth brought $250,000 to the first generation, the second-generation partner brought two million dollars, and the third-generation partner brings twenty million dollars. Seth and the second-generation partner get 3 percent and 7 percent of the third gen-

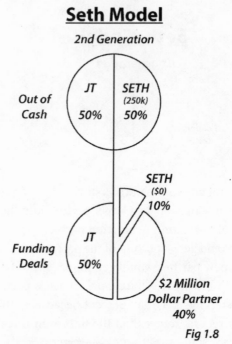

Seth Model

2nd Generation

Out of Cash

JT 50%

SETH (250k) 50%

SETH ($0) 10%

Funding Deals

JT 50%

$2 Million Dollar Partner 40%

Fig 1.8

eration partnership, respectively, for connecting JT to the twenty-million-dollar partner. The twenty-million-dollar partner gets 40 percent of the proven partnership and brings all of the cash to the third generation.

SETH MODEL THIRD GENERATION

Seth is out of cash, and the two-million-dollar partner is out of cash. The two-million-dollar partner attracts a twenty-million-dollar partner. Seth and the two-million-dollar partner both get ongoing royalties on the relationship for connecting JT to new twenty-million-dollar partner.

50 percent, J. T.
3 percent, Seth
7 percent, two-million-dollar partner
40 percent, twenty-million-dollar partner

In the fourth-generation partnership, Seth is out of money, the two-million-dollar partner is out of money, and the twenty-million-dollar partner is out of money, so the twenty-million-dollar partner brings in a

Seth Model

3rd Generation

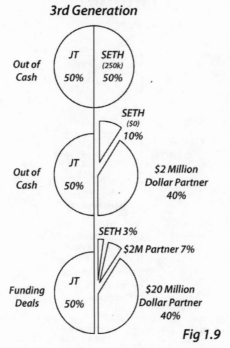

Fig 1.9

two-hundred-million dollar partner. The split is different on this level because the dollar volumes get so large, but everyone still gets paid for loyalty and bringing the partnership together.

SETH MODEL FOURTH GENERATION

Seth is out of cash; the two-million-dollar partner is out of cash; and the twenty-million-dollar partner is out of cash, but attracts a two-hundred-million partner. On this generation, J. T. takes a smaller share because the twenty-million-dollar partner is so valuable that he is rewarded with 15 percent of the partnership.

40 percent, J. T.
2.5 percent, Seth
2.5 percent, two-million-dollar partner
15 percent, twenty-million-dollar partner
40 percent, two-hundred-million-dollar partner

Seth Model
4thGeneration

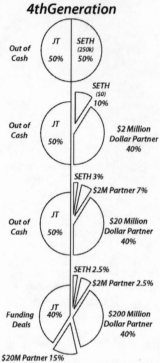

Fig 2.0

The Seth Model is effective for many reasons. Firstly, it rewards every single person who connected J. T. along the way with ongoing royalties. This makes pre-existing investors happy to refer new money in their network to the partnership and allows the partners to continue to make money even though they are out of cash. Everyone loves to be rewarded along the way, and it helps to keep all involved engaged and in the partnership for life. Secondly, the Seth Model works well because it allows working partners like J. T. to access higher social circles that he normally wouldn't have access to. J. T. started with virtually no cash, and Seth had social access to people with large amounts of money. In life, it's not what you know; it's who you know that makes the difference. It is always the biggest partner's responsibility to attract the new largest partner to the group because people with money know people with money. This allows the capital pool to grow exponentially, and everyone wins.

WHICH GENERATION GETS FIRST ACCESS TO A NEW DEAL?

The first generation partnership always gets first access to a new deal that becomes available. However, if the first generation partnership is out of cash, then the second generation gets first access. Third generation gets third priority and fourth generation gets last priority. Having a deal priority system rewards the people who invest first by giving them first choice on new deals. However, these first-generation partners have smaller and limited amounts of cash to invest, so they are usually maxed out. Partners cannot add more cash to their generation without bringing a new partner on, or this would be unfair to future generations. For example, Seth cannot suddenly invest five million dollars and steal all of the action from the future partners. He invested $250,000 and cannot bring more capital into the relationship to intercept the best deals from the other partners. Loyalty is the most important part of the Seth Model.

In my business, I have changed my thinking 180 degrees from my initial outlook. Rather than having a large base of investors, I would rather have a small number of partnerships for life. It makes more sense to reward loyal partners who have been with you since day one and allow them to connect you to further sources of funding. In my opinion, tight, profitable partnerships are more favorable than a large impersonal investor base that requires mass communication and management to maintain.

Relationships are always more valuable when you consider the total lifetime value of a reciprocal relationship. When you take on partners, make them partners for life, and reward these partners generously when they add value to the business.

Action Step: Make a list of ten people you know who could potentially invest with you. Make a guess as to how much they would have available to invest and gauge their level of interest. Who out of the ten people is connected to people with money? Who are the top three people you would like to invest with?

Chapter 9

SANDMAN EMPIRE: BUILD AN EMPIRE WHILE YOU SLEEP

"We have this notion in America of the Lone Ranger/Batman type—you know—someone who takes on the world alone. But in reality, all successful people need help. We need advisors, coaches, lenders, customers, and clients. True we ourselves have to do the work, but our 'team' that we put together—makes it all worthwhile. The sooner we realize this, the sooner we can reach our goals." —Robert Shemin

Although many entrepreneurs enter the field of business alone, achieving success in just about any field is impossible without a team.

This is especially true in business where "Lone Rangers" get squashed on a daily basis by teams of professionals.

1) The local "mom-and-pop" burger shop gets wiped out by McDonald's.

2) The local "mom-and-pop" hardware store gets crushed by Home Depot.

3) The local "mom-and-pop" department store gets destroyed by Walmart.

These small "Lone Ranger" businesses may provide better services than Walmart, they may provide better burgers than McDonald's, and they may offer more expertise than Home Depot. However, they cannot compete with teams of professionals that make up the talent at Walmart, Home Depot, or McDonald's.

One thing that separates "mom and pop" from the Walmarts, Home Depots, and McDonald's is that "mom and pop" have to sleep: Walmart, Home Depot, and McDonald's don't.

Kevin O'Leary, a Canadian investment guru, once said that he likes investments that earn money while he sleeps.

Investors make decent returns when their money grows during business hours. However, the same investors get rich when their money keeps working for them after they have gone to sleep.

In real estate investing, many investors don't consider themselves entrepreneurs. Most investors manage their own properties, hammer their own nails, paint their own walls, lease their own suites, and pick their own deals.

Most real estate investors don't get ahead, because they're too busy pinching pennies at the ten-dollar-per-hour level to make serious dollars at the CEO level.

In order to break out of the ten-dollar-per-hour mentality, it's up to the entrepreneur to break the link between time and money.

Most of us are taught from an early age that

> Time = Money

In reality, time does not equal money:

> Sales = money
> Assets = money
> Brand = money
> Press = money
> Information = money

When time equals money, we are stuck in an advanced form of slavery. We must trade hours for dollars. The problem with this model is that we only have twenty-four hours in a day and cannot make money while we sleep.

SANDMAN EMPIRE

(noun) An empire of business or real estate created passively through a joint venture or partnership between a passive money partner and an active working partner. The active working partner handles all aspects of the business, and the money partner is only responsible for financial backing. The passive partner is removed from all operations and can essentially sleep; hence the word "sandman."

Investors who can create a "sandman empire" can earn serious returns in a completely passive way and have unlimited earning potential; investors who fail to create a "sandman empire" are limited by time, focus, management, skill sets, and capabilities.

But how can we create a "sandman empire"?

In investing, there are two types of investors: active investors and passive investors.

Active investors are essentially entrepreneurs. They pick their own deals, manage their operations, manage their contractors, and run the enterprise. Naturally, these entrepreneurs get the highest returns possible, and in many ways, they take a risk on themselves to perform and run the enterprise profitably. Active investors may or may not invest money into their enterprise. But they invest their entire lives into the business instead.

Passive investors are more like silent partners who park their money with an active investor. Silent partners trust the entrepreneur to run the enterprise profitably. Silent partners need to be proficient at analyzing people and deals. These passive investors are the ones who get the benefits of building a "sandman empire" if they can select the right entrepreneur to grow their money.

Usually, passive investments have lower returns than active investments. However, passive investors can get much higher returns by partnering with an entrepreneur or an active investor and splitting the profits.

If a passive investor can find the right active partner, the possibilities are endless. When financial backing is paired with time and talent, tremendous value and profits can be created.

However, if the active partner is not chosen correctly, massive financial destruction can occur, including losing the investor's capital or worse.

A passive investor must perform proper due diligence on their active partner before "taking a leap of faith" and making a final decision to place their money with this person.

THIRTEEN QUESTIONS THAT MUST BE ASKED BEFORE PLACING YOUR MONEY WITH AN ACTIVE PARTNER

1) Does the active investor have experience with these types of assets? Not all real estate is created the same; single family homes are different from small multifamily ones, and small multifamily homes are different from large multifamily ones.

2) Does the active investor (AI) have experience with this strategy? Buy-fix-sell is different than buy and hold; make sure that your partner has relevant experience.

3) How do we recover if things don't go according to plan? Are there contingency plans in place if things don't go right? Has your partner thought of this scenario?

4) Has the AI lost money before? How did they handle the loss?

5) What is the track record of the AI? Does it show success? Are they hiding anything?

6) Has the AI built an adequate team? Can the team handle the additional business that the passive investor is funding?

7) How has the AI handled himself when things have gone wrong? Can he turn bad luck into good luck?

8) What transparency is offered? Who is doing the bookkeeping?

9) What options does the passive investor have to exit if things don't go right?

10) Does the AI have good personal relationships? Is he loyal, and in what way?

11) What is the brand of the AI? What does he stand for?

12) Is the AI 100 percent focused and committed to the venture, or does he have a day job? Do you want a "weekend warrior" managing your money?

13) What is the X factor for this AI? What makes him the over-the-top best choice for your dollars? Are you investing in someone who takes care of the details and provides an excellent product and experience? Or just another "real estate guy"?

If an active investor can provide satisfactory answers to all of these questions, then that person is a prime candidate to build a "Sandman Empire."

Of course, you will have to trust and verify all of the answers to make sure that the "walk" matches the "talk." When it comes to money, people will say whatever they have to in order to get your dollars. Don't be a victim of bad due diligence; put your potential partner through extensive scrutiny, ask the hard questions, and make sure you have a competent, trustworthy partner to build your empire while you sleep.

Action Step: Print out the thirteen questions that must be asked before doing business with a joint venture partner, and interview your current partner or potential future partner before moving further in your relationship.

Exclusive Bonus: Go to MoneyPeopleDeal.com and watch the bonus video "Sandman Empire—How To Create Wealth While You Sleep." The password to access your bonus is "insiderbonus."

Chapter 10

BUILD A BRAND OR DIE
A COMMODITY

Why should I invest with you? This is a question every new real estate investor is asked when raising capital. The question is blunt and brutally honest, and when I started in the business, I used to hear it all the time. As I became more established and really focused on building my brand, I heard this question less frequently because my brand answered the question for me.

In every market, whether it's electronics, real estate, food, clothing, or automobiles, the market will always attempt to force every single company and product into a commodity. Commodities are price driven, like coffee or sugar, and the consumer only wants the lowest price. Walmart is an example of a business that has done a brilliant job of forcing most products into commodities. Consumers shop at Walmart because they can get nearly every product for less; "Save money. Live better." is Walmart's slogan. Walmart is so good at forcing the price down on every single product that when they enter a new market, they virtually wipe out all competitors because they can offer the cheapest commodities. The market is always forcing great companies into commodity status. Fickle consumers are always hungry for the cheapest commodity possible.

Brands are the complete opposites of commodities. Fifty years ago, if a young entrepreneur came up with the idea of selling five-dollar cups of premium coffee and becoming a worldwide leader in coffee sales, people would have laughed at him. However, within the last twenty years, Starbucks® has done a brilliant job of turning a fifty-cent commodity like coffee into a zealous coffee culture with a worldwide following. Starbucks® coffee drinkers are fanatical; they will go out of their way and pay outrageous prices for designer coffee products. These coffee-drinking zealots are not just addicted to the coffee, but more so to the coffee culture, the social statement, the neighborhood meeting place, the free Wi-Fi, and the brand that Starbucks® stands for.

BUT HOW DOES A COMPANY OR A PERSON BECOME A GREAT BRAND?

Great brands are built over time, and a brand can be defined in a few different ways. Great brands are the emotional experience that a customer gets from first contact all the way through the sales cycle until the customer become a client and is retained for life. Brands are the corporate version of a relationship between a customer and a company; these relationships are deeply felt, instantly recognized, and are based on beliefs.

THE KEY QUESTION FOR A BRAND IS: HOW DOES THIS COMPANY MAKE YOU FEEL?

No matter how smart, how cold, or how calculated we think we are, humans are entirely emotional creatures. Great brands illicit instant emotions and instant reactions from us. Brands speak to our belief systems and either pull us in or repel us away if our beliefs do not align. Consider the following brands, as described by the first five words that come to my mind:

Starbucks®: High-end coffee, local meeting place, rich coffee smell, people on laptops using free Wi-Fi, trendy.
McDonald's: Fast, cheap, clean, open twenty-four hours a day, family.

Apple: Cool products, cutting edge, beautiful aesthetics, easy to use, high end.

Walmart: Low prices, large selection, open twenty-four hours a day, great return policy, convenient.

Donald Trump: High-end real estate, luxury, success, money, *The Apprentice*.

Coca-Cola: Fun, family, youth, energy, sex.

I chose the above six companies because of

1) Their visibility—everyone should recognize the six brands above.
2) Their size—all of the above six brands are leaders in their categories.
3) Brand equity—all of the above companies have enormous brand equity. Trump can license his brand name out to other developers and earn royalties without actually developing real estate.

HOW MUCH BRAND EQUITY DO YOU HAVE?

Brand equity is more important in today's economy than ever before. With the Internet forcing most companies into commodities, we must work harder than ever before to differentiate ourselves and create a great brand and experience for our customers. Building brand equity or brand value is the key to building a great brand, and I am conscious of building brand equity every day.

SIXTEEN WAYS TO BUILD A GREAT BRAND

Branding by Association: One of the easiest ways to create brand equity for yourself and your brand is to be associated with companies and products that share a similar message and feeling. If you are in real estate and have a picture of you hanging out with Donald Trump, the picture would create a considerable amount of brand equity because your associates would see you with a real estate celebrity and associate you with celebrity status and all things Donald Trump. This can be great for brand equity in real estate. People love celebrity and treat you like a celebrity when you associate yourself with the right people. Branding by association also works when joining the appropriate organizations, groups, and clubs in your field.

Traditional Media: One of my favorite ways to build brand equity is to get in the media. They say that any press is good press, and I would agree with this statement. Early in my real estate career, I was featured on the front page of the business section in my local paper. Just being featured in the newspaper improved my credibility, validated me in my field, and helped me raise money early on. Recently, I won an award for Joint Venture Partner of the Year, and *Canadian Real Estate Wealth* magazine did a four-page article about my business and my personal story. The value of having four full pages in a magazine is likely between $10,000 to $30,000 if I were to advertise, but having the brand association with a prestigious, well-distributed magazine in my niche is priceless.

Social Media: I love social media for building a brand because it's cheap, fast, and effective. Facebook, Twitter, and LinkedIn are all very popular, and it is very easy to create visibility and credibility on these channels. Social media allows you to create a fan base and lets people "reach out" and interact with you. This channel is very powerful because consumers these days expect to interact with their favorite brands, celebrities, and companies.

Google-ability: What happens if I google your name or your company's name? If nothing shows up on a Google search, then by today's standards, you either don't exist or you look like a fly-by-night scam. It's extremely important that you have a professional and credible looking Google search if someone searches your name or your company's name.

Logo/Website/Business Cards: Having a basic corporate kit with a decent logo, a clean website that looks professional, and clean, professional business cards is a basic way of saying that you are in business and that you are a professional. If you don't have a decent corporate kit, credibility and brand equity are severely hurt.

Personal Image: Look the part; dress the part. If you are a plumber, dress like a plumber; if you are a professional real estate investor, dress like a professional. Upgrading to a professional wardrobe is one of the easiest and fastest ways to increase your personal value and brand value all at the same time. I recommend spending some time and money on personal image.

Articles/Blogs/Literature: Either broadcast other people's articles and blogs through your social media accounts or create your own. Nothing positions you as the expert more than producing and distributing relevant information about your field. The one who controls the information in the market, controls the market.

Public Speaking: When you speak in front of an audience, you automatically become an expert on your topic and a leader in your field. This is one of the fastest and best ways to brand your company and yourself.

Well-Documented Track Record: A well-documented track record of success is one of the best ways to prove that you "walk the talk" and silence any doubts about your expertise. As a real estate investor, I keep pictures of every deal, usually before and after, and recently I have started recording my deals on video and distributing them on YouTube.com to create Google-ability and further branding.

Consistency in Business Dealings: This may sound elementary, but the biggest part of having a brand is being consistent. Little things like showing up on time, following up on communications, having a properly prepared presentation, and saying please and thank you go a long way. Master brand builders understand that the little things count and consistency is everything. Pay attention to every little detail of your brand; make sure that it represents the message you're trying to send.

Belief Selling: Understand what your brand stands for, who you are, and what you stand for. Understand your belief system, and communicate it through your brand. Statements that begin with "we believe" are very powerful and speak to the emotional core of an audience. Define your belief system, and use it to sell on every front.

Publish a Book (or e-book): Published authors are the "author-ities" in their fields. The moment you publish a book, you become an expert in your field. Consider the fact that 98 percent of the top 1 percent wealthiest people in the world have authored a book, whereas only 2 percent of the average earners have books. If you're not ready to write a full fifty-thousand-word book, take some time to put together a short e-book and quick start your brand.

Have a Story: Define your brand with three stories that you can use depending on what image you want to portray. Facts tell, and stories sell; people buy stories before they buy you. Tie your story in with your company and your brand, and you create very powerful meaning. Many ultra successful companies have stories that are compelling, entertaining, and inspiring. Consider the story of Steve Jobs from Apple, a college dropout who started out building computers in his garage and went on to become the founder of the first $700 million company in the US (according to *Fortune* magazine). The story is great, the company is great, and the Apple brand is the most respected brand in the world.

Have a Feeling: Define a feeling that you want people to feel when they are around you. When I am selling suites or homes I have renovated to flip, I want my customers to feel rich. The homes and suites are not necessarily luxurious, but I want my customers to feel like they are purchasing luxury. For people, feelings are stronger than reality. Establish a great feeling, and make sure the feeling is maintained throughout your buyer's experience.

Social Proof: Although I think testimonials are kind of "old school," they work! When other people validate you through a written testimonial, a video testimonial, an introduction, or a referral, it creates a powerful effect and position for your brand. Humans are social creatures, and we are always looking for people who are validated by others. Keep a collection of testimonials and video testimonials, and ask for introductions. These can be very powerful if used correctly.

Charity: As an extension of belief selling and branding by association, charity is a great way to show what your brand stands for. McDonald's elevates its brand by helping families through Ronald McDonald House, which improves the lives of sick children. This charity serves to strategically increase sales with families. If McDonald's associates itself with families, the brand increases in value and families eat at the restaurant.

If, on the other hand, they gave to a charity associated with obesity, heart attacks, or cancer, sales would likely plummet.

When you have a great brand, every part of the business is easier. Before I started building my brand, I had to cold-call to raise money. Today, money comes to me more easily than ever without cold calling. Deals come to me daily because people know where to send the deals. Great people who are leaders in their fields want to work with me because they can see the value and message of my brand. Investors refer other investors to me because they know that I can deliver the goods and make them money. When I started in the business, I had investors complain about my fifty-fifty split; now I don't have any investors complain, and I also cut my split to sixty-forty in favor of myself. When you are branded, you can charge what you want because you have determined your own value; you are no longer a commodity. Your customers will either pay the price or they won't. Apple does not offer discounts on their products. They know they are the best; they charge for the best, and the customer gladly pays.

I have the philosophy that even if I make zero dollars at the end of the year, I want to have every action performed in the year to build my brand equity. That way at the end of the year, I have a multimillion-dollar brand. In many ways, the brand is more important than the business, because a great brand can attach any number of businesses to it easily and make profit, but it is much harder to take a business and turn it into a brand. Great brands take time to build, and although they are intangible, they have real balance-sheet value.

Cherish your brand, build your brand, and guard it with your life. Your brand is your identity; it's the way the public perceives you, and if you defile your brand, it is impossible to get back.

Action Step: Evaluate your brand according to the sixteen brand-building techniques above. Find your three strongest branding opportunities and your three weakest areas for development.

Exclusive Bonus: Go to MoneyPeopleDeal.com and watch the Bonus Video "Build a Brand or Die a Commodity." The password to access your bonus is "insiderbonus."

Part 2

THE DEALMAKER, THE MIND-SET, AND WHO YOU MUST BECOME

This section focuses on the mind-set you must develop and the person who you must become in order to be a dealmaker. This section is mostly conceptual and focuses on attitude, because entrepreneurship is 99 percent mind-set. In life, success is built on attitude, not aptitude.

Chapter 11

PAYING THE PRICE
FOR SUCCESS

When people ask me, *How do I get into real estate investing?* the best answer I can offer is: *Work for free.*

The response I usually get is, *I can't afford to work for free! I have bills to pay! I'm worth more than that! I'm educated. I don't work for free! I belong to the union! I'm too busy!*

The second answer I can offer is: *Pay someone to teach you.*

The response I usually get is, *But training is too expensive! I can't afford to pay someone! Training is a scam!*

The third answer I can offer is: *Buy a house, make every mistake in the book, and learn from the school of life.*

The response I usually get is, *But I don't know what house to buy! I don't want to make mistakes! Mistakes are expensive!*

The truth is that I have built my career in real estate by using all of the above methods. I have worked for free, I've paid for training, and I've ignorantly bought a house and learned the hard way from the school of life. All three methods are very good, and all have contributed to what I have become today.

Years ago, when I decided I wanted to become a professional real estate investor, I attended every free event I could find. I saved up 70 percent of my income to purchase books and attend real estate seminars. At first I volunteered at some of the events, performing menial tasks like setting up chairs, selling books at the back table, crossing names off lists, showing up early, and leaving late. I also volunteered on and off for one of the leading companies for a three-year period. Eventually I was hired to work for the company after three years of volunteering and being rejected twice for the job. I even flew and drove to other cities while volunteering just to be a part of the team. Eventually, the founder of the company approached me to hire me to work for him; ironically, I had been hired a few days earlier by his staff.

While working for one of the leading financial education companies in Canada, I learned invaluable skills such as setting up events, raising capital, selling, stage presentations, telemarketing, hiring, and firing. The education I got was invaluable, the opportunity was fantastic, and the knowledge I took home with me after working for the fortieth fastest-growing company in Canada would make me wealthy.

However, the key to my success and my education was working for free. Had I failed to work for free, I would not have absorbed the skills required to become a full-time real estate entrepreneur.

Working for free is the litmus test for finding a winner and weeding out the losers. A winner will persist; a loser will give up after a few hours. Every week, men and women who want to be mentored in real estate approach me and ask if I can mentor them. I used to offer them a position on my team because I understand how hard it is to find a mentor. I would offer them a position making calls or finding deals. However, after wasting my time with scores of uncommitted people, I now charge for mentoring. The serious pay; the curious walk away.

There are only three ways to get ahead in this world: work for free, pay for training, or try to succeed alone and make your own mistakes.

If you want to be rich—work for free. The knowledge and connections you will gain are priceless.

If you want to find a winner to be on your team, find someone who will work for free or someone with a history of working for free.

Throughout history, humans have learned skills from a master-and-apprentice type of relationship. Formal schools and universities did not exist. If you wanted to be a blacksmith, you apprenticed under the blacksmith for free. If you wanted to be a potter, you worked under the potter. If you wanted to be an artist, you apprenticed under an artist. This was the way of life; there were no entitlements, no credentials, just experience earned from trading time for information.

When considering taking on deal partners, contractors, assistants, designers, or anyone onto your team, ask for a free trial period. If the person you are going to work with will not work for free, chances are you do not want to work with them. Either fire them or proceed with caution. People who are not confident enough with their product to offer it for free as a trial are not worth associating with.

Action Step: Make a list of skills that you want to learn. Then make a list of people who could teach you these skills, and offer to work for free. Start off with working one day a week for an undefined amount of time. Let your mentor know they can fire you at any time if they aren't happy with you. Offer so much value that they cannot refuse.

Chapter 12

BECOMING UNSTOPPABLE

"It's the unconquerable soul of man, not the nature of the weapon he uses, that insures victory." —General George Patton

Real estate investing, like any business, has a high failure rate. Nine out of ten businesses fail within the first five years, and nine out of ten of the survivors fail in the second five years of operations. In my own business, virtually every part of the business has failed at some point, and every part of the business has recovered and been repaired. In real estate investing, there are countless forces that work against you to stop you from success; to succeed in the business, you must become unstoppable.

Why are some people absolutely unstoppable, while others quit at the first sign of difficulty? Why do some people manage to make it to the gym every morning, while others only show up on January 1 and quit by January 7? Why do some marriages fall apart after the five-, ten-, fifteen-, or twenty-year mark, while some last "until death do us part"? Why do immigrants who come to a new country with nothing manage to get rich, while others born with every advantage slip into poverty?

The people who manage to push through adversity all have one thing in common: they have a strong *why*.

A wise man once said, "Some men have thousands of reasons to fail, but they only need one reason to succeed."

Simon Sinek, a brilliant speaker, educator, and researcher, created a simple, yet powerful concept called the "golden circle." The golden circle very simply illustrates the difference between people with a strong "why" and people without a "why."

Simon Sinek's Golden Circle

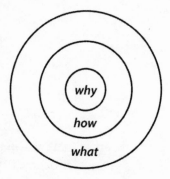

Fig 2.1

Simon wanted to know what the difference was between an average person and an exceptional person. What he discovered was that behind every person, organization, or business, there is a *why*, a *how*, and a *what*.

The average person, business, or organization focuses on the *what* first, the *how* second, and may never address the *why*. These people work from the "outside in" and focus externally.

The exceptional person, business, or organization focuses on the *why* first, the *how* second, and the *what* last. These people work from the "inside out" and focus internally first.

Inside out vs. Outisde in

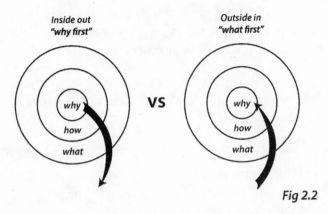

Fig 2.2

The results between the average and the exceptional are both shocking and yield completely different results.

Consider two computer companies: Apple and Dell.

On one hand, communication from Dell operates from the outside in:

1) *What*: We make great computers.
2) *How*: They are beautifully designed and easy to use. Want to buy one?
3) *Why*: Undefined.

Communication from Apple, on the other hand, is from the inside out:

1) *Why*: With everything we do, we believe in challenging the status quo.
2) *How*: The way we challenge the status quo is by making computers that are beautifully designed and easy to use.
3) *What*: We make great computers. Want to buy one?

To compare the results of Apple to Dell in the last five years, Apple has become the most respected brand in the world many years in a row and the most valuable company in history, while Dell has fallen off the radar.

The golden circle can easily be applied to fitness as well. The average person approaches the gym on January 1 every year with the following mentality:

1) *What*: I want to get fit this year and lose some weight.
2) *How*: I am going to buy a gym pass.
3) *Why*: This is my New Year's resolution.

This person is usually delinquent on gym attendance by the time February rolls around, because a New Year's resolution is not a strong enough reason to ensure success.

The exceptional person approaches the gym with the following mentality:

1) *Why*: I must go the gym consistently to create and maintain the body I desire. This is integral to my self-image, self-esteem, and personal success.
2) *How*: I will go the gym every day.
3) *What*: I will have a fit and healthy body that reflects my self-image, self-esteem, and personal success.

If I were a betting man, I would bet on the "exceptional" person every time for success because the why is much stronger and I know that the mission will be accomplished.

When you compare the emotional strength of a New Year's resolution vs. my personal self-esteem, the latter will win every time because it is a much stronger emotion than an arbitrary goal set at a New Year's party.

When the golden circle is applied to marriage, it is very easy to see which married couples will "make it" and which ones won't. Divorce rates are at an all-time high right now because many people set up their marriages with the following mission:

1) *Why*: We're getting older, balder, and fatter; we both want to raise some kids before it's too late.
2) *How*: We will get married because marriage is required to have kids.
3) *What*: Lets have some kids; aren't they wonderful?

This relationship will last at a maximum sixteen to twenty years because these people got married on the premise of raising kids. As soon as the kids are old enough to leave home, the marriage usually fails because the marriage was not built on the premise of a primary relationship. The bride and groom are not committing to each other—they are committing to the kids.

A stronger marriage that would last "until death do us part" would be

1) *Why*: We are in this relationship to help the other person become the best they can be. My partner spiritually complements me, and I spiritually complement him or her.
2) *How*: We will spiritually commit to each other, make it official, and get married.
3) *What*: A spiritual union between two committed people through marriage—children may or may not happen.

The reason to succeed needs to be greater than the reason to fail; if the why is strong enough, then success is ensured.

Unfortunately, finding the why in our businesses, personal lives, and relationships is not an easy task. When I meet people who are highly motivated to succeed in their businesses, I usually see one of two reasons why they are motivated for success:

1) They are a parent who wants to spend time with and or help their children become successful.
2) They are a child who wants to take care of and help their parents.

There are many reasons why we want to succeed, but in my experience, I have seen these two reasons most frequently in the people I meet on a day-to-day basis.

As for myself, I came from a family that fell apart over money. Virtually every problem in my family came from not having enough money, and because of these problems, I want to make sure that my family is taken care of in the future. I never want to find myself in the position that my parents were in where they separated, fought over money for eight years, and then finally divorced. Life is too short, money is too easy to make, and it isn't worth the pain that everyone suffers. Neither of my parents knew how to "create money"; they only knew how to work for money. After watching my parents split up over not having enough money, I decided I would make it my mission to learn how to create money.

"Money is not the root of all evil, lack of money is the root of all evil."
—*Rich Dad* by Robert Kiyosaki

Many of us may be in our businesses or personal endeavors for the wrong reasons. If you are in a business or relationship for the wrong reason, correct the mistake; establish a new *why*, and watch your success reach new heights.

Remember that a man can have thousands of reasons to fail, but he only needs one reason to succeed.

Action Step: List the *why, how,* and *what* for your business. How can you emotionally charge your mission to make yourself unstoppable?

Chapter 13

LAYING BRICK OR BUILDING A CATHEDRAL

To be an entrepreneur is to be a visionary. Henry Ford had a vision of everyone in America owning an automobile. Steve Jobs had a vision of everyone in the world owning and operating a computer that was easy and delightful to use. Mark Zuckerburg had a vision of connecting everyone in the world easily and efficiently through a social network. All of these men had great visions that preceded their inventions, and they all changed the world.

"Imagination is more important than knowledge." —Albert Einstein

Two men are laying brick, and one man is miserable. He lays brick after brick and curses each brick as it's laid upon mortar. The other man is excited and filled with joy to be laying the exact same brick.

What makes these two men different?

One man has vision: he is building a beautiful cathedral.

The other does not: he is merely laying brick.

These men are identical men, performing an identical task in an identical way, but one is energized and overjoyed, while the other is miserable and depressed.

I recently hired a coach to take my life and business to the next level. The first thing my coach had me do was fill out my "vision board." I was unprepared for a vision board because I had not spent much time creating a vision for my business and myself.

After being assigned to create a vision, I started to spend serious time constructing the vision that would fuel my life and my business.

What do I want my life to look like? What do I want my home to look like? What do I want my health to look like? What do I want my bank account to look like? What do I want my workday to look like?

The list goes on.

Vision is so powerful because once we have a great vision, we can literally reverse engineer our reality from the blueprints of a great vision.

Just like the example of two men, one can see the lines of a cathedral in his vision, and this man feels like he is contributing to a larger mission and a beautiful creation. The other man can only see bricks and mortar. Each brick he lays is painful; his body is exhausted, and he works like a slave.

Which man would you rather be?

After becoming more conscious of vision and spending some time to create my own "vision plan," I realized we all have very different visions of what we want our lives to look like. Sadly, though, most people have no vision at all for their lives and just accept whatever comes easily to them.

When someone asks me for advice, I always ask what their vision is.

It startles me to find out that very few people have visions for their lives. Most people are satisfied with just laying brick. Only a very select few are building a cathedral.

Many people have goals, hopes, and dreams, but few have a vision. The vision, in many ways, is more far more powerful than transactional goals, baseless hopes, and actionless dreams.

The reason why I prefer a vision plan to all of the above is because a vision can be dissected and reverse engineered into small, actionable steps that can be executed each day.

Goals are one dimensional, hopes are for the hopeless, and dreams are for dreamers. However, a strong vision that has been reverse engineered into daily, actionable steps will quickly become a reality.

We must create the vision of our cathedral and then begin laying brick— one brick at a time.

If we are consistent and persistent in our "bricklaying" actions, eventually our cathedral will begin to manifest, and the vision will come to life.

The people with the strongest visions are the leaders in all facets of life. Visionaries like Steve Jobs, Gandhi, and Henry Ford all saw the world differently and worked toward their vision.

Through a powerful vision, reverse engineering of that vision into a blueprint, and execution of the small actionable steps of the blueprint, the world can be changed one "brick" at a time.

The future belongs to those of us with strong visions, clear blueprints for achieving the vision, and a specific plan of daily actionable steps.

Action Step: In your life today, are you laying brick or building a cathedral? If you are building a cathedral, whose cathedral are you building? Your own? Or someone else's?

Chapter 14

DEAD MONEY

If you were offered $35,000 a year to sit at a toll booth and collect change from cars crossing a bridge, would you take the job?

Or would you decline and look for the next opportunity?

What if you were paid $100,000, $200,000, or $300,000 for the same task? Would you take the job?

What if you were paid $1 a year to sit at the same tollbooth?

Personally, I would not sit at the tollbooth for any amount of money, because money earned at the tollbooth is "dead money."

We are human "be-ings" not human "do-ings."

Daily tasks that help us become the person we want to become create life, energy, and success. These tasks have purpose, feed our spirits, and nourish our souls; by performing tasks we enjoy, we become the person we want to "be."

If a task or job does not bring us closer to the person we want to become, we earn dead money and, in some ways, waste our time, effort, and energy.

Eventually, if you earn enough dead money, getting out of bed in the morning will become an insurmountable challenge.

Dead money is a term I learned from Raymond Aaron, a *New York Times* best-selling author. Raymond explained that the money he earned from his published books that were unaligned with his core purpose were "dead money." In some ways, these books hurt his brand, wasted years of his life, and were very expensive in opportunity cost.

In my own business, I make sure every action I take advances my career by building brand equity or by earning cash and brand equity. If I am able to monetize my actions and build my brand equity at the same time, I make the biggest gains in spirit and in my bank account.

My mentality is that I succeed even if I earn zero dollars at the end of the year, but have built a million-dollar brand through my business activity. Steve Jobs paid himself a salary of $1 per year while he was the CEO at Apple because his mission was to build the company and put a dent in the universe. I have a similar philosophy to Steve Jobs, whom I have idolized since sixth grade, when he returned to Apple and unveiled the original iMac in the late 1990s. He immediately became my hero for his vision, and I kept a magazine with his picture on my desk at school.

I am fortunate enough to be aware of my brand and purpose. The average person does not consider his brand, his brand equity, who he is, who he wants to become, or where he is going in life. For the average person, this is very unfortunate. Brand identity is one of the greatest opportunities we have to capitalize on our values and talents and become a bigger, better version of ourselves.

Most people are stuck in "dead-end" jobs that are either high paying or low paying, and every dollar they earn is a "dead dollar." The dollars they earn do not build their dreams or advance their careers.

If you earn enough "dead dollars," the dollars you earn will eventually build the bars of an emotional prison.

Money is a medium of exchange and is called currency because it needs to move in order to be relevant and useful, like electricity or water. Consider the terms used to describe money; they relate to water: cash flow, liquidity, illiquidity, inflow, outflow, and currency.

If money stops moving, money dies.

If people stop moving for long enough, people die.

If the spirit stops moving, the spirit dies.

If you are earning money in your career but are not moving toward becoming the person you wish to become, your career and spirit will eventually die.

Years ago I used to work Frito-Lay, the company that makes Lay's chips and Doritos. I used to put chips on shelves at Walmart every morning at 4 a.m., and I earned a disproportionately high salary for doing so. Walmart employees stocking chips at 4 a.m. were making $8 per hour; I was making closer to $20 per hour to do the exact same task.

However, every dollar I earned was dead money.

The money was dead because, although I was earning money daily, I was not advancing toward my goal of becoming an entrepreneur. The money was good, but my soul was dying. I was becoming a professional shelf stocker and not a professional entrepreneur. I was not advancing toward the person I wanted to become. The life I wanted was not being built with my actions, and consequently I was earning dead money that did not help me in my pursuit of happiness.

Many people think earning money in itself is a good return on time, but in fact, earning dead money is a complete waste of time, waste of spirit, and a waste of life.

Would you rather live a life of poverty doing what you love or a life of comfortable indifference?

Most people will say they would rather do what they love and live in poverty. However, 70 percent of people are not happy with their current jobs or current careers.

This means that 70 percent of people earn dead money every day.

A wise man once said, "Talk is cheap; it takes money to buy the whiskey."

What this wise man was saying is that most people say whatever makes them sound good (*I would rather do what I love*), but most people's actions do not align with their words.

Remember: talk is cheap, and money buys the whiskey.

I'm not saying we should choose a life of poverty out of passion to pursue what we love. I'm a firm believer that we can "have our cake and eat it too."

I think it's 100 percent possible to do what you love, monetize it, and become rich.

I believe you can have it all: happiness, love, and money. When it comes to happiness, love, and money, there is always enough for everyone.

Obtaining happiness and money is a topic of major study for myself at this time in my life. What I find is that the more I love my career, the more I love my daily routine, the more fun I enjoy, and the more money I make.

> Fun = money
> Love = money
> Enthusiasm = money
> Money = life

The more fun, love, and enthusiasm I enjoy, the more life I have, and my wallet benefits as well.

I have abandoned the pursuit of "dead money," and if a task or job doesn't line up with my mission, my vision, and who I want to become, I will not perform it.

Do what you love, and the money always comes.

Complete the mission, and the money always comes.

Provide enough value, and the money always comes.

Money is a result of a job well done; it is an effect, not a cause. Actions performed at a level of excellence equate to money earned. Money itself can never motivate someone to be better, achieve excellence, or create more value, because money intrinsically has no value.

Money is intrinsically dead; we are the ones who breathe life into money. People are the ones who attach external value to money, and we use it to build our dreams.

Money is neutral, and money doesn't care. Money doesn't cry for you when you are sad, and money won't drink champagne with you when you want to celebrate.

Money will, however, buy you a bottle of champagne to celebrate.

Money can either be alive or dead depending on how we earn it. It is up to us as the wielders of money to respect the neutrality of money, breathe life into money, and allow money to flow through us in our personal pursuit of happiness.

Money, life, spirit, happiness, enthusiasm, and joy are all currencies, and we must allow them to flow.

If we allow money, life, spirit, happiness, enthusiasm, and joy to flow through us, we will become congruent. We will prove our integrity, and the universe will reward us for respecting its laws and creating abundance.

If we shut off our spirit, enthusiasm, and joy, then we also deactivate the spiritual power of money and the power of life.

If we deactivate the spiritual power of money, the money we earn will die the moment it touches our hands. Instead of using our earned money to build our dreams, our dead money will build an emotional prison around us where we are forced into slavery for the almighty dollar.

When we align with the person we want to become, we earn the Midas touch, and everything we touch turns to gold. When we are out of alignment, we lose our Midas touch.

Ask yourself, *Do my daily actions help me become the person I want to become? Am I earning dead money? What is my purpose? How am I achieving my purpose?*

We all have the Midas touch if we can find our purpose deep down inside of ourselves. Respect money as a tool; respect the neutrality of money and the power of money. Allow money to live, and money will let you live the life of your dreams.

Disobey money, kill money, and you will find yourself in financial prison. Don't let money die.

Protect money, and it will protect you.

Action Step: Write down the different ways that you are currently earning money in your life and business. Which sources of income are dead money? How can you change your dead income to living income?

Chapter 15

THE THREE PILLARS
FOR ACHIEVEMENT

In the early 1900s, an author by the name of Napoleon Hill was commissioned by Andrew Carnegie (the steel magnate) to interview the top five hundred richest people in the world and discover the common formula for great riches. After many years of hard work, Napoleon Hill published his masterpiece, *Think and Grow Rich*. The book contained the formula for great riches, and Napoleon Hill became very wealthy himself by teaching people around the globe the secret to creating great wealth.

Throughout history, many people have searched far and wide for the formula for riches. Some people would call it the philosopher's stone (the stone that could turn lead to gold) or the fountain of youth.

The truth is, Napoleon Hill's formula for great riches is both a philosopher's stone and a fountain of youth. It can turn lead (or even thin air) into gold and can also preserve youth and beauty if used correctly.

Man has scoured the earth for these arcane abilities, and yet everything a person needs to know about turning air into gold and endless youth is written in the pages of *Think and Grow Rich*.

Relatively recently, a Canadian entrepreneur and author by the name of Doug Vermeeren studied the formula for wealth and decided to do a modern study of Napoleon Hill's work.

Doug interviewed the top five hundred achievers in the world, including CEOs of major corporations, sports stars, actors, athletes, and many types of people that were excluded from Napoleon Hill's list (which was made up of mostly industrialists, inventors, and entrepreneurs).

Throughout his study, Doug was able to add extra insight to Napoleon Hill's work, and in some circles Doug Vermeeren has been given the title of "the modern day Napoleon Hill."

I recently had the privilege of spending a day with Doug Vermeeren, and I was fortunate to have him pass on some knowledge to me. One concept that Doug shared was "the three pillars for achievement." He found that there are three things top achievers all have:

The Three Pillars for Top Achievement

> 1) Affectionate, loving parents
> 2) A supportive partner/spouse
> 3) A deep religious faith

The common denominator between affectionate, loving parents; a supportive partner; and a deep religious faith is that every one of the "pillars" supports the achiever in the mental, physical, emotional, and spiritual realms.

In other words, the top achiever is not succeeding alone, but has extra support in all aspects of life. This person has the power of many, but is perceived as succeeding alone.

To paraphrase T. Harv Ecker, money is created in the physical realm because it is a "print out" of who we are in the mental, emotional, and spiritual realms.

Wealth and riches are created inside of us in intangible realms, and the results are manifested through physical success. We see the results of the wealth physically, but do not see the mental, physical, emotional changes, shifts, and support systems that manifest physical wealth, money, and success.

When we examine the three pillars for top achievement, we can easily see why top achievers have a higher probability of success if they possess all three pillars.

Affectionate, Loving Parents: Affectionate, loving parents are very important for top achievers because parents form the base of a child's self-esteem. Self-esteem is crucial to becoming a top achiever because it allows a person to take a risk. I call self-esteem "emotional capital," and people with high self-esteem are able to take risks and withdraw from their "emotional bank accounts." People with abusive parents or absent parents may have depleted emotional bank accounts and will have a much harder time taking risks. Unconditional love from a parent is important when taking risks because the risk taker will know that no matter how bad they fail, their parents will always be there to support them emotionally, physically, mentally, and spiritually.

A Supportive Partner: When Warren Buffett was asked to give advice to a graduating class of Ivy League students, he bluntly offered one pearl of wisdom: "Marry the right person." When a top achiever is going to "put it all on the line" and chase their dream, they require their partner/spouse to do one of two things:

a) Actively pursue the dream with them *or*
b) Passively support their partner emotionally, physically, mentally, and most importantly, spiritually

Top achievers will go through hell and back to become the best in their field. There is an unwritten law in physics that states, "When you push on the world, it pushes back," and oftentimes, people who pursue excellence in their field are met with great adversity at every turn. Whether it is jealous peers, rivals, or other unsavory people, the road to the top is not easy. Emotional and spiritual support from a primary relationship is absolutely essential for success to take place. Without this key support, a person will easily be crushed when faced with enough pressure and adversity. A supportive spouse will make a top achiever twice as strong and twice as resilient when "the world pushes back." If you are single, make sure you heed Buffett's advice and marry the right person.

A Deep Religious Faith: Faith is a key ingredient to great success and achievement. I have shifted my spiritual belief system many times in my life but have always retained one key factor called "faith." Faith is an extremely important part of success because faith allows a person to make leaps in logic.

For example, if you want to be the best salesperson in the country, but have not made any sales yet, logic would tell you that your outcome of becoming the best salesman in the country would be very unlikely. If you listen to logic, you will always give up without trying.

However, if you feel it in your heart, guts, mind, body, and soul that we you will become the best salesperson in the country, then faith will allow you to leap over the logical argument and pursue your vision with burning determination.

Faith is one of the most powerful techniques that top achievers use because it can help us to achieve things that are unbelievable, improbable, and superhuman. Faith allows us to harness the greater, invisible spiritual forces around us that some would call "the power of intention," "infinite intelligence," "the universe," or "God" and use these forces to achieve our wildest dreams against all odds.

WARNING: Although faith can be extremely powerful in the positive sense, faith itself is a double-edged sword. Faith allows the user to leap in logic, which can be used in a positive way to achieve greater goals with no prior experience. However, faith can also leap logic in the wrong direction and create a closed-off mind that can completely cripple a thinking mind. Use faith wisely and consider the cause and effect of such a wildly powerful tool. As the label often reads on potent substances, read the manual. Consult a professional, and use with extreme caution.

Although we often see success in its physical manifestation, true success is first created in the nonphysical realms of the spiritual, mental, and emotional. Only once "inner" success has been found can "outer" physical success be manifested through wealth and riches.

Having a strong support system in the intangible realms through loving parents, a supportive spouse, and a strong religious faith are the foundation of the structure that is required to reach the stars and become a top achiever.

Like grass, relationships require watering and maintenance. Take care of your relationships, water them, fertilize them, manicure them, and watch them grow. Consistently be mindful of your support network; treat your support network better than gold, and your results will be startling. In the end, no one succeeds alone, and great relationships can make the difference between wild success and crushing defeat.

Action Step: Take a moment to compile an inventory of your life and your support system. Ask yourself, *Which parts of this system do I have today?* and *Which parts are lacking?* Find ways to strengthen your deficiencies and create stronger relationships.

Chapter 16

IF YOU WANT TO BE RICH, WORK FOR FREE

One day I spent the day in Edmonton with one of my business partners at the Fast Track Super Conference hosted by Darren Weeks. Darren is the Canadian "Rich Dad," one of my mentors, and a man who taught me a lesson that has made me successful to this day. I owe much of my success to Darren because I developed a skill set that very few people have (and one that is almost impossible to obtain because so few people teach the art of raising capital). When I worked for Darren I learned 1) how to sell and 2) the art of raising capital.

Darren Weeks is an extremely successful Canadian entrepreneur. His company, the Fast Track Group, has been in the top one hundred fastest growing companies in *Profit Magazine* three years in a row, and when I worked for Darren, his team was the fortieth fastest growing company in Canada. In my opinion, Darren's greatest personal strength is his ability to identify and assemble groups of amazing people with unbelievable talent who are motivated by a spiritual mission greater than the individuals in the group.

Contrary to traditional business models, The Fast Track Group was built around giving rather than getting. Darren prided himself by giving out "more education than anyone in the industry." There are few businesses that have been built on giving first and receiving second.

Darren provides more free value to the market than anyone else. To some people, giving out free information and building a business around it sounds insane, costly, and risky . . . but I think the modern consumer expects free gifts and services before they buy. This is the trend in the market today, and with the Internet generation dominating the market-place, it will continue for decades to come.

Business models that revolve around *free* gifts and services are especially strong in the financial and real estate sectors right now.

When I was twenty-two, I attended the Fast Track Super Conference in Edmonton, and I was absolutely blown away by the caliber of the compa-ny. I loved the mission, I loved the people, and I loved what the company was doing for Canadians. I wanted to be a part of the group. I could feel the energy, and it was infectious.

One thing Darren always used to preach when he was educating his au-diences was, "If you want to get rich, work for free." He would often pick out a young man or woman in the audience who would be just entering the work force and ask them, "Can you afford to work for free?"

Almost every time, the young man or woman would say, "Absolutely not!" and then Darren would teach the lesson.

The difference between the rich and the middle class or poor is that the rich do not work for money; instead, they work for free. This may sound completely ridiculous, but let's consider two scenarios:

In my personal life, when I was in my early twenties, I had two jobs at two different times. At my first job I worked for money; at my second job, I worked for free.

MY FIRST JOB AS AN EMPLOYEE (WORKING FOR MONEY)

At age twenty-two I worked at Frito-Lay Canada as a merchandiser (which is a fancy word for putting bags of chips on the shelves at four in the morning at Walmart).

My primary motive for working with the company was the salary and the hours. I was truly chasing the dollar in every sense of the word. I wanted a salary so I could get mortgages to buy real estate. I took that job for the wrong reasons, I didn't learn the proper skills in the field, and it became harder and harder to get out of bed every day when I worked there. I had no passion for the industry and felt there was nothing to learn.

When I left the company, I had maxed out my purchasing power for real estate but had acquired zero skills or intellectual capital toward building my own business. Since I had chased the dollar, I had a small cash reserve on hand; however, I had built no skills and no contacts in real estate. Although I had made a little bit of money, I had no human equity in myself, no skills, and no way of propelling myself forward toward my goals, hopes, and dreams. In a way, I had traded time for money, lost my time, and intellectually crippled myself.

Most people don't consider the skills they learn at work. My advice to young entrepreneurs is to leave their job once they stop learning the skills offered in the position. Always work to learn. Move from job to job until you have all of the skills required to run the business of your choice.

Lesson: When it comes to work, *never* chase the dollars. Find what excites you; find where your heart is and chase your passions. The money doesn't matter, and it always gravitates toward the most enthusiastic people.

MY NEXT JOB (WORKING FOR FREE)

I had heard Darren Weeks say on stage, "If you want to get rich, work for free." I took his advice, although it challenged my belief system. I had nothing to lose, so I volunteered for his company whenever he was in town.

Every time Darren was in town, I would dress up in a suit, show up early and leave late, pack and unpack books, process paperwork, seat people, help out with sound production, and do any task that was required of me. I expected no financial compensation and just wanted to be on the team.

I volunteered for Darren for three years, and I applied to work for his company three times. Twice I was rejected for the job, and the third time I applied, I said, "I have been volunteering at this company over the past three years. I have applied twice and been rejected. I will keep applying until you hire me."

I then flew to Edmonton and volunteered at a Fast Track Super Conference event shortly after my interview. Darren Weeks noticed I had flown from Winnipeg to Edmonton to volunteer to work for him. After the event, he personally took the time out of his evening to offer me a job with the company.

What Darren didn't know was that I had already been hired to start work with the company, and on the following week I was to begin formal training.

Consider the lesson: working for free and volunteering had grabbed the attention of the founder of the company and had brought me onto the team of my choice.

Now that I was positioned in the only company I wanted to work for, I got paid to learn more about the industry I was passionate about—I was in heaven.

I got paid to sharpen my skills and become an extremely valuable asset to myself. I learned the art of sales, how to do public presentations, how to run an office, how to recruit good employees, how to fire bad employees, prospecting, sales tracking, databases, securities regulations, and public speaking.

Most importantly, I learned how to raise capital and work with investors. This has been my "secret sauce" in my business, and it's what sets me apart from other real estate investors who *do not* have the skill set.

These skills are the base of my empire and the building blocks of my portfolio. I have based my entire career and current business around skills I acquired by working for free.

Had I not volunteered at the company first, I would have had no chance of working with them. I would have been of no value to their tribe, and

I would not have learned the skill set that makes me valuable today. Had I not volunteered, I would still be a wandering soul stocking bags of Doritos on the shelf at Walmart at 5 a.m. I would have throttled passions and big dreams, but no way of executing them or aligning with other people who matter.

Lesson: Every week I meet young people who are passionate about a certain field or career. Many people say they are passionate about music, art, acting, sports, television, radio, etc. and don't know how to break into those "hard to enter" industries. Whenever I study a highly successful person, I notice that almost all of them worked for free, scrubbing toilets, mopping floors, or doing the most menial jobs at the bottom of the barrel just to be a part of the industry of their choice. Unfortunately, young people today do not see such opportunity.

"Flipping burgers is not beneath you, your grandparents had a word for flipping burgers; they called it opportunity." —Bill Gates

Steven Spielberg began his brilliant career in film by just "showing up" to the movie studio, wearing a suit, and pretending to be a director in an abandoned office. He was a film student who pretended to work at the studio and snuck in every day. The people at the studio assumed he worked there, and eventually his passion for film brought him an opportunity to make his first film.

Steve Jobs of Apple was too poor to pay for his college education, so he collected aluminum cans on campus and would cash them in to eat his next meal. Jobs had no money, so he would sit in the university classes for no credit and let his mind absorb the information. The free classes he attended for zero credit hours became the building blocks of the Apple philosophy. Steve was a genius who blended liberal arts with technology. If he were paying for the classes and chasing marks/credits, he would have likely been focused on the grades and not the knowledge; Apple computers could look very different today—or not exist at all.

Trent Reznor, the front man of the iconic band Nine Inch Nails, got a job as a janitor at a recording studio where he mopped floors and poured coffee for countless hours a day. He shared an apartment with a friend and ate nothing but peanut butter sandwiches to survive while he recorded his debut album in the middle of the night at the vacant studio.

The most brilliant people in the world, the people who are at the top of their game and dominate their fields with enthusiasm, passion, and leadership, often started at the bottom, working for free.

The reasons why working for free is so powerful are

1) It gets you in the door; an employer can't say no to free labor.
2) You make contacts in the industry of your choice immediately.
3) You learn the business from the "ground up."
4) When a job opens up, you are first in line because you are at the business and eager to work anyway—you are the best choice!
5) If you aren't passionate about the industry, you won't last long; you will weed yourself out to find your true passion.
6) Over time you gain experience, and the company you are volunteering for *or a competitor* of theirs will hire you. This is a no-lose strategy if you stick with it.
7) You free your mind from "chasing the dollars," which can limit your creativity. You will approach the industry with a creative, fresh perspective. This is priceless in the long run.

When I was in the music industry, I used to say, "You know you're in the right industry when you can work eighteen hours a day, lose money, and still wake up the next day to do it all over again." Follow your heart, and make a choice of passion and not logic when it comes to work.

To paraphrase Canadian multimillionaire and founder of Boston Pizza, Jim Treliving, make decisions about money with your head, decisions about people with your gut, and decisions about work with your heart.

Even if I lost everything tomorrow, even with no skills, no money, no contacts, and no experience, I would rediscover what I am excited about and offer to work for free in the industry. Of course, I would need some income to live, so I would get a job at McDonald's for eight hours of the day (or another McJob) that is not too stressful, then work for the company of my choice for free in the other eight hours. I would continue this eighty-hour-a-week routine until I secured the employment of my choice, and then I would quit my McJob. I would then gain all of the skills

I need to be successful in my choice industry and reevaluate my position. I would likely find a way to start my own business in the same industry and leave as fast as possible as soon as I stopped learning.

Action Step: Take a step back from where you spend your time on a daily basis. Then ask yourself, *Am I chasing dollars? Or am I building valuable skills in an industry of my choice? Is my work based on passion and enthusiasm? Would I keep working there if they stopped paying me?*

Chapter 17

THE NO-CASH DIET: KILL THE ADDICTION TO MONEY

Mind-set is perhaps one of the most important assets in real estate investing, business, or entrepreneurship.

Most people think money is holding them back from reaching their dreams, but in fact, money does not exist. The only thing holding people back from reaching their dreams is their mind-set.

When I was twenty-two, I made the choice to go into real estate investing. I had literally no money and no experience. All I had was passion, a gut feeling that real estate was where I wanted to go, and a very strong reason why I wanted to pursue real estate.

The little money I did earn as a guitar teacher was invested primarily in real estate education, seminars, and books. Since many of these educational seminars are extremely expensive ($1,500 to $30,000) and all of my cash from my job went into funding my education, I learned how to operate my real estate business and my other businesses with no cash.

I was on the *no-cash diet.*

If I found a property I wanted to buy, I was unable to buy it because I had no cash and often no credit, so I had to raise the money. I had to learn how to "bootstrap" and keep my operating budgets razor thin. I also had to learn how to motivate and keep team members on the team and working for me with no cash. None of this is particularly easy to do, but I was forced to learn the skills because my passion told me to go into real estate and I "jumped in" feet first.

Cash is never a problem for me today in my business because I started with no cash, have operated with no cash, acquired all of my property with no cash, renovated buildings with no cash, motivated teams with no cash, travelled with no cash, and have learned how to live with no cash.

My mind-set has transformed from a "cash-required" mind-set to a "no-cash-required" mind-set.

Many people who get into real estate or business think that they need cash for all of the above. I think their mind-set is lazy.

Most people think that business is like walking into a McDonald's and buying a Big Mac. If they want the Big Mac, they have to buy it with cash. If they don't have cash, they can't buy the Big Mac. Nothing could be further from the truth. There are many ways to get a no-money-down Big Mac, but you need to be creative.

Unfortunately, having cash makes you lazy in your mind-set, and although I am excellent at operating with no cash, I am not immune to the laziness that comes with having cash.

Whenever I have a windfall profit and suddenly "have cash," I quickly find out how stupid I can be as I spend my windfall profits on thoughtless, meaningless purchases. I don't go out of control, but I definitely notice that my intelligence goes "down" when my personal cash goes "up."

Understand that money is a drug; the more you have—the more you want. If you have none, money cannot control you. It's very liberating.

In the movie *Wall Street 2*, there is quote I will never forget. One man asks the other, "How much money do you want?" His answer was, "More!"

We are all programmed to be the same. We always want more money.

We have some . . . then we want more. If we have more . . . we *still* want more. There is no end to the madness, and the only cure for the "more" disease is a no-cash diet.

In ancient times, fasting or taking all food out of a person's diet for a few days was a way to purify the body of addictions. It was a way to keep the mind in control of the body and not have the body control the mind with cravings and addictions.

Today we have lost the idea of fasting for the most part and let our addictions rule our decision-making. Money is no different. To stop a money addiction, you must fast from money—go on a no-cash diet.

Of course, choosing to be on the no-cash diet is scary and socially disturbing. Many people would rather die than live on the no-cash diet. The truth is that I am no different. I hate being on a no-cash diet because it's very painful. However, as Dr. Nido Cubein says, "Pain is mandatory, suffering is optional."

Throughout my life, my passion has forced me into situations where I had no options but to go on a no-cash diet to chase my dreams because I literally had no other options.

I wanted to participate in real estate as an investor as a young man, not an old man, and refused to become a Realtor®. I bought the home study course to become a Realtor® three times and never had the stomach to open it. My only option for pursuing my passion was to operate as a real estate investor with no cash.

Since starting in real estate, I find myself in situations over and over again where I'm operating a business that is hopelessly undercapitalized, but I know how to work the business and grow it to be successful because I have lived on the no-cash diet.

The best way to get on the no-cash diet is to literally quit your job, have no plans of ever getting another one, and start up a business on nothing but guts and passion. However, I do not recommend this for anyone; there is extreme risk with doing something like this. Plus, your spouse/ significant other will hate you and potentially divorce you.

I quit my job with no plans of ever becoming an employee again three times, and twice I was forced back into a job because I could not assemble a proper business.

The decision to go on a no-cash diet is a big one—a decision that 99 percent of people never choose to pursue because they favor comfort and security over freedom.

Truthfully, many entrepreneurs get themselves into stupid and risky situations that force them into a no-cash mind-set. I don't think anyone is really born with this mind-set, because it's too abstract to comprehend. Usually the mind-set is created through a combination of the following:

1) Failure
2) Bankruptcy
3) Job loss/quitting a job
4) Starting a business blindly on passion
5) Over leveraging to pursue a dream

All of these situations have a pain threshold associated with them and have their own risks. However, if you find yourself going through some of those experiences listed above, you will find out that once you get over the initial shock of getting out of your comfort zone and exploring your deepest fears, you will find (if you are mentally tough enough to survive) that you do not need cash for any aspect of your life.

If you can survive through one of the more traumatic experiences above, you will see money for what it truly is. Money is intrinsically worthless paper, and it does not exist.

Money is an enslavement tool that governments print out of thin air when they need it. Why should governments be the only ones allowed to print money? Why don't you print some too?

Once you have removed yourself from being a slave to money and realize that you no longer need it, you will learn to become "the master of money" and see it as a tool to build and chase your dreams.

Although no one is born with a no-cash diet mentality, children who become entrepreneurs often come from parents who are either: (1) dead or (2) incompetent. Dead or incompetent parents force children into a no-cash diet early in life, and the children never become addicts of the money drug. These types of children become shrewd, creative, and are often wildly successful.

Off the top of my head, three multimillionaire entrepreneurs who had dead or incompetent parents are

1) Fred Trump, Donald Trump's father
2) "Rich Dad," Robert Kiyosaki's alternate father
3) 50 Cent (Curtis Jackson)

Those of us who learn the no-cash diet early in life are the ones who have the most time to build and reach for their dreams. I had the luxury of being forced onto the diet at age twenty-two, while many of the men above were forced onto it at age eleven or twelve. No matter what your age, consider what a no-cash diet is and how you can emulate one to free yourself from the money drug that rules 99 percent of the population.

Exclusive Bonus: Go to MoneyPeopleDeal.com and download the bonus e-book *How to Start in Real Estate with Zero Dollars.* The password to access your bonus is "insiderbonus."

Chapter 18

THE LUXURY OF NO OPTIONS

"The grass is always greener on the other side, until we get to the other side and realize that it requires watering and maintenance too." —Dr. Nido Qubein

Focus brings clarity to the mind. Focus brings success. Focus brings happiness.

Happiness in life is determined by what we focus on and choose to think about. If we are focused on our passions, obsess over them, and think about them all day long, we live very happy and productive lives.

However, the enemy of focus is options.

Have you ever noticed that some of the least happy people are the ones with the most options?

The media is littered with rich and famous celebrities who have all of the options in the world: they can live where they want, spend their time how they want, eat what they want, drive what they want, have the house that they want, and have the means to completely design a perfect life. And yet, many people who "have it all" are miserable and pursue hard drugs to escape reality at all costs. These people have too many options, and when the mind has too many options, focus erodes along with sanity and happiness.

In my own life, I have had periods where I had "too many options," and from the outside, it would appear that I was on top of the world. Surprisingly, on the inside, too many options bred discontent, unhappiness, and even mild depression and anxiety.

When we think we have too many options, we always ask, *What if I had gone the other direction?* or *What if had chosen differently?* or *What if I had dated that other girl?*

What if . . .

Eventually, the mind tears itself apart, focus decays, and we are left in a sea of what ifs with no commitment or focus on any one thing.

On the flip side, there are people in the world who have the "luxury of no options." We see people in marriages who have "no option" to get divorced, and they work on their problems until they find happiness in the relationship. We see people in businesses who have "no option" to quit, and these people frequently reach success because failure is not an option. We see people in life who have "no option" of an alternate path, and they become the most wildly successful people in their fields because they have the luxury of no options. All of these people have the highest levels of focus and absolutely zero chance of defeat.

When Julius Caesar landed on the shores of Britain to wage war with the British tribes, he ordered his men to "burn the boats." His troops would either be victorious, or they would all die in battle—no one goes home a failure. Caesar gave his men the luxury of no options, and he was victorious in his campaign.

The Spartan warriors of ancient Greece had a similar mentality. Death before dishonor was a mantra that accurately described the Spartan war machine, and they were known throughout history as the most battle-hardened, persistent, fearsome, victorious, disciplined warriors of all time. The Spartans created a culture based around the luxury of no options, and this culture created a brand of warrior that is still studied in modern military schools and will continue to be famous for ages to come.

When we look at the most successful business people, a common element for entrepreneurs is that they find themselves in a no-options situation early in life. Usually, successful entrepreneurs have parents who are either dead or incompetent, and they have to take over the family business at a very young age. This was true for Fred Trump (Donald Trump's father) as well as Robert Kiyosaki's "Rich Dad." A modern example is Curtis Jackson (50 Cent).

Other entrepreneurs who find "the luxury of no options" choose a path in life at a young age and give themselves no way to retreat.

I was reviewing the Thirty Richest Drummers in the World list, and two names that stuck out at me were Tre Cool of Greenday with a net worth of $45 million and Dave Grohl of Nirvana and the Foo Fighters with a net worth of $225 million. Both Dave Grohl and Tre Cool dropped out of school at age sixteen to play punk music. They had the luxury of no options, burned the boats, and had no way of reversing their choices.

The luxury of no options brings clarity and extremely powerful focus to the mind. A focused mind will always find a way to achieve a clear, well-thought-out vision.

Where most high school dropouts are perceived as derelict losers who wander through life, three of the greatest entrepreneurs of the information age were all dropouts: Steve Jobs (cofounder of Apple), Bill Gates (founder of Microsoft), and Mark Zuckerburg (Facebook founder). These men all made a choice in university to burn the boats and choose the "luxury of no options."

In my own life, the happiest, most exciting, most relevant moments have all been moments where I had put myself into a no-options situation.

I was forced to leave the corporate world (something many people struggle with) because if I didn't quit my job, I would be bankrupt in three months. Even while earning a nice, comfortable salary at my job, I would have still been bankrupt if I had stayed. With the luxury of no options, I quit my job and woke up every day with the intention of finishing my failing real estate development. I was 110 percent focused on finishing the development at all costs and did not leave the job site daily until it was too dark to work.

Life becomes very simple and fulfilling when there are no options. Every morning, the only thing I thought about was finishing the development. Every afternoon, the only thing I thought about was the development, and every evening, the only thing I thought about was the development.

I was immersed in my work; my focus was crystal clear. Failure was not an option, and I was happier than ever before. What is more interesting is that my chance of failure dramatically dropped to zero. There was literally no chance for the project to fail once I had found the luxury of no options.

My contractor's truck was broken, so we couldn't haul materials. I loaded up my small four-door sedan with doors, toilets, and vanities (none of which fit in a small car) and drove around town to six different suppliers to get the necessary supplies to the job site.

My general contractor, who had mentally given up on finishing the project, was amazed I was hauling large building supplies in a small sedan and not a truck. I drove my small car with door slabs, lumber, and vanities sticking out of the passenger windows and the trunk. I had to take back roads so the police wouldn't pull me over.

We had no labor to paint the building, so I put on my painter clothes and painted every day myself, while also hiring anyone I could find in the online classifieds to paint. I also attracted friends and family to help with the labor because I had found the luxury of no options, and everyone could see the high-stakes game being played and the importance of my success.

Somehow, I successfully completed the project within forty-five days of quitting my job (I had ninety days to complete it). From that experience, I learned some of the most valuable lessons of my life so far:

    1) When a person has their back to the wall and has no options, the failure rate for that person dramatically drops (almost to zero) and the success rate dramatically increases (almost to 100 percent).

2) When a person has no options, their focus level skyrockets. They become obsessed with succeeding. All distractions and procrastination are silenced.

3) Every obstacle becomes a nonissue because the motivation level of a person with no options is inhumanly strong.

4) A person with no options can achieve superhuman feats that the average person with options will marvel at.

As a real estate investor, I frequently see part-time corporate people who want to make a "smooth" transition into full-time real estate investing. For many people, quitting the corporate world and taking full control of one's time is major desire. However, this desire is often not strong enough to actually put together a concrete plan and stick to it.

My own passion and desire were so strong that I put myself in a situation where I found the luxury of no options by accident and became successful by default. Failure was not an option for me because I literally had no options—it was live or die.

I feel the pain of the people who badly desire full control of their time and want to leave the corporate world in a "smooth" way. But after studying success, I'm not sure if there really is a possibility of a fast and smooth transition.

I'm fully convinced there's a slow and smooth way, but I'm not sure if that method will satisfy the soul's hunger for freedom.

To paraphrase the words of Robert Kiyosaki, we can only choose one of two things in life: security or freedom. Those who choose security end up with maximum security, which in turn is a maximum-security prison. Those of us who choose freedom end up with maximum freedom, which is zero security.

For the men and women who find themselves with the luxury of no options, they only have one choice, and that is freedom at all costs. Any security they once had has been obliterated, and there is only one chance for survival. Freedom is the only choice for these people, and they pursue it with a life-or-death vigor that is infectious and absolutely unstoppable.

Action Step:

1. What would you give up to have "the luxury of no options"?
2. Have you ever found yourself in a "no-options" situation? What was the outcome?
3. What do you value more: security or freedom? Which are you currently pursuing?

Chapter 19

CROSSING THE MINEFIELD TO WEALTH

In 2013, I had the pleasure of spending some time with Doug Vermeeren. Doug is a very successful entrepreneur who has studied and worked with four hundred of the world's top achievers. Fox News calls him the modern-day Napoleon Hill because he has studied the secrets and formulas for wealth. He created the sequel to the movie *The Secret*, called *The Opus*, and was able to turn one dollar into one million dollars in six months.

When I, along with my colleague Shaun Furman from *Millionaire Mentors*, helped Doug set up an event in Winnipeg, he shared the short questionnaire he used to interview the top four hundred achievers in the world.

One question that I felt was extremely relevant to wealth generation is

A million dollars' cash for you is on the other side of a field of explosive land mines. What do you do?

    A) Stay put.
    B) Make a run for it, and hope for the best.
    C) Go slow and steady.
    D) Follow someone who knows the quickest and safest route.

My initial reaction for what I have done in the past was B (make a run for it). In my career, I have earned my education at the "school of life" and have paid my tuition with blood, sweat, and tears. I have stepped on a few "land mines" on my journey and, fortunately, have not been wiped out by doing so.

THE FOUR WAYS TO CROSS THE MINEFIELD TO WEALTH

Option 1: Stay Put

If a million dollars were sitting on the other side of a field filled with explosive land mines, most people would stay put. For most people, any sort of risk is too much risk, and they would rather have total safety and security. Unfortunately, you cannot become wealthy by just "staying put." You must take action, make moves, and make mistakes to cross the field. People who stay put never become wealthy.

Option 2: Make a Run for It, and Hope for the Best

Making a run across a field of land mines, regardless of the reward, is absolutely reckless. You cannot "make a run," take a blind risk, and "hope" that it works out. Hope is for the hopeless. People who "make a run" in real life will take on so much risk that they end up getting hurt or financially wiped out. Some of these people may start risky businesses that they do not understand or "put all of their eggs in one basket." Although this strategy could pay off, and pay off big, I do not personally recommend it. I have made a few "runs" in my life and have risked everything on some deals. In hindsight, making a "run for it" has far too much risk, and there are so many better ways to cross the minefield of wealth.

Option 3: Go Slow and Steady

Going slow and steady across the minefield is much lower risk than "making a run for it." However, you may not be able to cross the field in time. Time is the most important currency in life and in wealth. Wealth is not actually measured in dollars, but in time. If you spend all of your time being cautious and not crossing the field fast enough, you may never cross it. Caution is always important in the pursuit of wealth, but we need to balance caution and action so we get to our destination on time.

Option 4: Follow Someone Who Knows the Safest Route

Finding a coach or a mentor who has crossed the field is the option that most wealthy people have chosen to build their wealth. This is the option I have chosen to pursue (after trying to "make a run for it"). Coaches and mentors can show you where the land mines are. They can also show you where they have failed and can get you across the field safer and quicker than you could alone. *However*, there is always a cost associated with the advantage of having a coach. Usually you have to pay your coach or mentor either in time or money.

NOTE: Paying for success in time or money is much easier than paying in blood, sweat, and tears. Mistakes can be very costly, and the stress is never worth it.

Find the person who has what is needed to cross the minefield, and find out what they need to educate you. Life is very simple when you understand who you are, what you want, and who can help you get "across the field."

I find it interesting that most wealthy, successful people all answer the previous question the same way. There is a formula and a code for wealth, and when you study enough people, you can see there is no such thing as luck and success is a choice.

Action Step: In life, we are all faced with a minefield that stands between where we are today and where we want to be. The two questions we must ask ourselves are

     1) Who will help us cross the minefield to wealth?
     2) What will you pay to get to your destination?

Coaching programs are available at MoneyPeopleDeal.com.

Chapter 20

PRESSURE MAKES DIAMONDS

"Pressure makes diamonds."—General George S. Patton.

What do you do when you are under pressure? Do you crack? Do you fold? Do you avoid and hide from the world? Or do you stand up, get stronger, and push harder to persist?

Pressure makes diamonds . . . but it can also crush people.

Years ago, when I attended my first real estate seminar, the speaker asked, "And what about stress? After you have made your money, do you think the stress goes away?"

Almost every hand in the room went up, and the room was silent.

After a long pause, the speaker continued, "Stress never goes away, and you must learn to manage it. Just because you have more money does not mean that you have less stress."

Throughout my life, I have constantly placed myself in high-pressure situations. I played music at a professional level, I was a national leader in direct sales, and I'm currently playing the highest risk and reward game in the world: entrepreneurship.

Somehow, I have always been attracted to high-pressure situations because I am naturally a competitive person and have always wanted to compete and work with the best.

For me, the pressure has always been necessary for me to push to the next level because I believe that pressure makes diamonds.

Of course, being under pressure is extremely uncomfortable, and it can take its toll on your sleep, your comfort, and your overall quality of life. But looking back on my life so far, the greatest, most exciting, relevant moments have been the ones of greatest pressure and greatest importance.

In contrast, my most unhappy, joyless, depressing moments have been the moments of absolutely no pressure.

We all remember the days of high school where we would have an exam in three weeks. Three weeks would go by, and we would neglect to study. Thirty hours before the exam, we would still neglect studying. Eight hours before the test, we would be up all night trying to learn advanced calculus while trying not to overdose on caffeine.

Somehow, pressure can bring out the best in people. Pressure brings clarity, decision, and action to people who normally have confusion, indecision, and passivity. Pressure shows us who we really are and can bring out the hero or the wimp inside of us. Pressure lets us know what we are made of and lets us know how far we can be pushed so that we can see where our limits truly are.

One of my favorite things about pressure is that it brings out our natural instincts. Instinct is not a common topic of conversation in our modern world because we think of feral cats, wild dogs, or rabid beasts as having instincts—not civilized people! Civilized people do not have instincts . . .

Or do they?

Kathy Kolbe is a theorist and educator who developed a test called the Kolbe A™ Index (Kolbe.com), a series of short questions that measure your instincts to show you what your strengths are when under pressure.

This information has been unbelievably helpful in my own life. It also explains why I am happiest under pressure—because I am forced to become my natural self.

Pressure brings out my natural instincts and allows me to pursue the "best version of myself."

My Kolbe A™ Index tells me that under pressure I "improvise." People with instincts similar to mine make great salespeople, public speakers, on-camera people, radio hosts, interviewers, storm chasers, video game designers, and nonconventional educators.

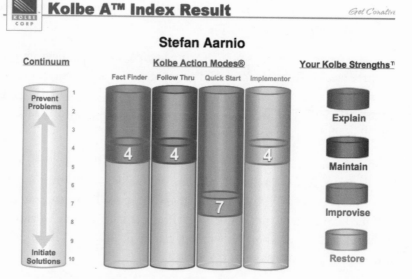

Kolbe A™ Index Result

Get Conative

Stefan Aarnio

Continuum	Kolbe Action Modes®				Your Kolbe Strengths™
	Fact Finder	Follow Thru	Quick Start	Implementor	
Prevent Problems					Explain
	4	4		4	Maintain
			7		Improvise
Initiate Solutions					Restore

Kolbe Action Modes are behaviors driven by your *instinct* -- **not** your personality or IQ.

Fact Finder: is how you gather and share information.	**Follow Thru:** is how you arrange and design.	**QuickStart:** is how you deal with risks and uncertainty.	**Implementor:** is how you handle space and tangibles.
Your way of doing it is to **Explain**.	Your way of doing it is to **Maintain**.	Your way of doing it is to **Improvise**.	Your way of doing it is to **Restore**.

Every ring on a Kolbe Continuum represents an equally positive trait

Stefan Aarnio
Kolbe Career MO+™ Report

Career MO+
4-4-7-4

Career paths based on your leading strengths

The following are examples of jobs that have brought satisfaction to people with an MO similar to yours.

ADVERTISING
PUBLIC RELATIONS
ON-CAMERA TV
SPECIAL PROMOTIONS
SALES
NEW PRODUCT DEVELOPER
COMEDIAN
THERAPIST
LOBBYIST
PUBLIC SPEAKER
RADIO INTERVIEWER
BUYER, GIFT WARE
SPECIALTY RETAILER
IMPROV ACTOR

CRISIS CENTER DIRECTOR
ALTERNATIVE PROGRAM EDUCATOR
INSURANCE SALES
DAY TRADER
LEGISLATIVE AIDE
INVENTOR
SPORTS AGENT
VIDEO GAME DEVELOPER
COPYWRITER
PUBLISHER
FUNDRAISER
MEDICAL DIRECTOR
STORM CHASER
INTERVIEWER

All of the above "careers" are high-pressure, performance-based paths that require little or no formal training to achieve success.

This would explain why I am least happy in low-pressure situations and most happy in high-pressure situations. Pressure forces me to become who I naturally need to become. Pressure is what turns coal into diamonds, and it also turns a raw, undeveloped, average person into a refined success.

I would encourage you to take the Kolbe A™ Index and find out what your instincts are and to find out how you work under pressure. Find out what your natural skill sets are, where you are happiest, and then focus your whole life and business around that skill set.

Personally speaking, I need to "improvise" all day long to feel fulfilled and happy. I have reorganized my entire business around allowing me to "improvise" while key team members around me handle all of the other tasks.

By pursuing this strategy, I have seen greater success, experienced more fun, and felt more excitement. All of this can be had from selecting the tasks and roles that excite my instincts

Action Step: Please take a moment to invest in yourself, learn about your instincts, and harness your talents. Go to MoneyPeopleDeal.com/Kolbe to take your Kolbe A™ Index!

Chapter 21

LIONS VS. GAZELLES

"Every morning in Africa, a gazelle wakes up. It knows it must outrun the fastest lion or it will be killed. Every morning in Africa, a lion wakes up. It knows it must run faster than the slowest gazelle, or it will starve. It doesn't matter whether you're the lion or a gazelle—when the sun comes up, you'd better be running." —Christopher McDougall

In every market, whether business, jobs, or investing, there are lions and there are gazelles. The lions are the fastest, strongest, fiercest animals in the field, while the gazelle is a fast, light pack animal that finds safety in numbers.

The lion represents the leader in the market: he feeds on his competition and swallows up the slowest, weakest gazelles. There are few lions, and only the best animals can become lions in the field.

The gazelles symbolize the "herd" of average players that flood the market and swarm the terrain in packs. Where one gazelle goes, the rest follow. Unlike the few lions on the field, there are scores of gazelles. As a gazelle, you do not have to be the best to survive. Instead, you must only be faster than your slowest competition to win another day of life.

The lion requires a complex skill set and a high standard of performance to live. He must become strategic while hunting and move in a complementary pattern to the herd. He must appear where the herd does not expect him if he is going to kill and live another day.

The gazelles only need an average skill set and average standard of performance. The herd feels secure when all animals are the same, and the gazelles organize themselves in a crowd. The crowd makes the gazelles feel safe because it gives them a thin veil of protection from the lions. This thin veil keeps the lion from focusing on any one gazelle, for the lion cannot catch them all. The lion can only catch one gazelle for his dinner and let the rest of the herd go. The gazelles know this, and they base their survival strategy around this fact.

As an investor or entrepreneur, which would you rather be? The lion or the gazelle?

Would you rather have the illusion of safety and move with the herd as a gazelle?

Or would you rather have the freedom of the lion to hunt and kill on your own terms?

In my investment/entrepreneurial career, I have always chosen to become the lion. In my opinion, the lion is a better choice in the investment/entrepreneurial world because I have always had a rule for myself: whatever the average person does—do the opposite of it, and you will succeed.

Most people are not successful at all, so if you do the opposite of the average person, logically, you will be a success.

If the average person wants to buy, then sell.

If the average person drinks, then don't drink.

If the average person smokes, then don't smoke.

If the average person has a 60-inch plasma screen TV, then don't own a TV.

If the average person has a PC, get a Mac.

If the average person doesn't exercise, then exercise.

The formula is quite simple, and it works more often than not.

People are pack animals, much like gazelles. As mammals, we flock and freeze when we are scared. We form packs to feel safe, and we want to belong to a group.

Unfortunately, groups don't know how to make decisions or create good ideas. Decisions and ideas come from an individual and never a collective.

A committee of professionals built the Titanic, while one man built the ark.

No matter which subset of the world or the market you look at, there is always a majority and a minority.

Pareto's principle states that 20 percent of your actions create 80 percent of your results. This relationship applies to markets and people as well. Eighty percent of the market is dominated by 20 percent of the players.

In the case of the lion and the gazelle, it would be more skewed. Perhaps the lions, as 5 percent of the animals, control 95 percent of the gazelles.

In America, 1 percent controls 99 percent of the world. This is exactly the same concept as the lions and the gazelles.

The question is, Why would anyone want to be a gazelle when you could be a lion?

The truth is that most people are not lions because it's easy and convenient to be a gazelle, whereas it is extremely difficult to become a lion.

The gazelles have safety in numbers; they do not have to be fast (just faster than the competition). They can feed on grass, which is plentiful, and at the end of the day they can go to sleep with a belly full of grass. They don't have to worry about hunting and killing because they can graze all day. Gazelles know that tomorrow will be the same easy routine, and they find security in the herd.

Lions, on the other hand, hunt alone or in very small groups. They have to be much faster than the slowest gazelle, or they starve to death. Lions cannot eat grass like the gazelle and require meat to survive. Every day the lion must be tracking and hunting for his next kill. If the lion fails to kill a gazelle, he goes to bed with an empty stomach, and too many empty stomachs in a row means death for the lion. The lion has no security and must be better than the gazelle to survive.

To be a gazelle is to be average.

To be a lion is to be a champion, a performer, and an athlete.

Every day, both the lion and the gazelle are running to survive. But what makes the two animals different is "who" they must be on a daily basis to survive.

In every business, every industry, and every market, there are lions and there are gazelles.

Every morning when you wake up, you must make the choice between running the field as a lion or a gazelle. No matter which one you choose, you are going to be running anyway.

Are you committed to being the best in your field and taking the lead as the lion? Or would you rather blend into the crowd and take your chances as a gazelle?

In the end, it doesn't really matter which animal you are. Either way, you will be running. But if you're running anyway, you might as well choose excellence and learn to be the lion.

Action Step: In five years you will be the same person you are today except for the people you meet and the books you read. Answer the following questions to determine if you are developing into a lion or settling for a place in the herd as a gazelle:

1) How many books have you read in the last twelve months to improve yourself, your business, or your position in the market?

2) How many coaches and mentors have you worked with in the past twelve months?

3) How many seminars, networking events, or conferences have you attended in the last twelve months?

If the answer to any of these questions is zero, chances are that you're turning into a gazelle and not a lion. To be a lion you have to constantly be on your game, learning and evolving to stay at the head of the pack.

Go to MoneyPeopleDeal.com and click on the link "Books That Change Lives" for a list of books that have shaped my life so far.

Chapter 22

TURNING PRO: ALIGN WITH PROS, CULL AMATEURS, BURY TRAITORS

One weekend I had the pleasure of flying to Edmonton with one of my partners to hear Robert Kiyosaki, author of *Rich Dad Poor Dad*, speak. Robert is over sixty years old now and has had some very hard experiences in the past few years.

1) He has severed ties with the founding partners of the Rich Dad Company. These people were stealing from him.

2) He was recently in the media for going "bankrupt" and was sued for breach of an agreement with his promoter, Learning Annex.

3) *CBC Marketplace* did a fairly slanted review of his education company recently and misrepresented his brand in Canada.

Life is not easy when you are on top—everybody wants a piece of you.

Even still, Robert is tough as nails and still able to evolve, grow, and innovate his business.

As an audience, we were treated to an entire morning and most of the afternoon of Robert sharing some of his most recent thoughts. Many of the things Robert taught were contextual and high-level concepts that have brought his life into a new level of focus.

Robert's talk pertained mostly to self-development and had very little to do with money at all. He talked about character, context, and personal growth (which is in my opinion more important than the nuts and bolts of money).

One book that changed Robert's life is called *Turning Pro* by Steven Pressfield.

Robert has a communication style through which he is able to take a hopelessly complicated subject and make it simple. For example, Robert can explain financial derivatives (a topic that no one really understands) by using the analogy of oranges: oranges are the asset; orange juice is the derivative. A box of oranges is a package of derivatives that were sold as an "investment." If the oranges in the box are bad, then the orange juice and the whole box of oranges are bad. This is how the American real estate bubble was built and collapsed after people found out "the initial oranges were bad." This analogy makes derivatives so simple a three-year-old could understand them.

People understand oranges, orange juice, and boxes, but they do not understand complicated financial concepts. This is why a few smart white-collar criminals can rob entire countries and no one goes to jail. It's also why Robert is the king of his field.

Robert shared a concept from the book *Turning Pro:*

In business or in life, there are three types of people: professionals, amateurs, and traitors.

1) Professionals are people who solve problems. These are the people you can call on and hire to solve a problem, and it is fixed without any hassles and is done on time and on budget. These are people you will want to call again and keep close to you. True professionals are worth their weight in gold; cherish them and keep them forever.

2) Amateurs are people who create problems. Amateurs are people who are in a field, but cannot fix problems with 100 percent satisfaction. They often fix a problem but do it incorrectly and create another problem in the process. These people are not professionals, because they do not practice the basics and

have little discipline. They charge the fees of a professional, they think they are professional, but they are not professional by any means.

3) Traitors are people who steal life. Traitors can disguise themselves as professionals or amateurs and steal money, time, and life from other people. They are often not conscious of their thievery and often mean well. However, either by incompetence, greed, or another character flaw, they end up stealing the lives of other people. The only way traitors can get what they want is by stealing from others.

Robert shared a story about a group of amateurs he hired to maintain his lawn. Robert paid the amateurs a cash deposit, and in few weeks, his lawn looked worse. He then asked the amateurs why the lawn was worse, and they said, "Pay us more money and it will look better." A few weeks later, the lawn looked even worse. Robert said again, "Why is the lawn worse?" The amateurs replied, "Pay us more money," once again. The cycle went on until the lawn looked terrible, and Robert fired the amateurs. At the end Robert was frustrated, having wasted money and time; he had a lawn that was nearly destroyed.

After Robert's lawn was almost ruined, he hired a professional and asked him, "What will it take to fix this lawn?" The professional replied, "Five thousand dollars and five months." Sure enough, in five months, the lawn looked absolutely beautiful. No hassles, no mess, on time, on budget. And Robert was extremely happy.

"Your life sucks when you are hanging out with amateurs and traitors; you give them money and you don't get results," Robert said.

Three quick questions you can ask a potential business partner to find out if he is an amateur, professional, or traitor:

1) What is your goal in your business or in working with me?
2) What are you willing to do to achieve this goal?
3) If the answer to number two is "nothing," then this person is not a professional and likely not the best asset to your team.

"Some of the biggest traitors (in society) are school teachers. They don't have the guts to resign," Robert said. "School teachers can steal and ruin more lives through miseducation and misinformation than any other person in society . . . worse off, they always get paid whether they do a good job or bad."

Professionals practice the rudiments of their art forms every day and strive to be better each and every day. Their goal is to become the best in their fields, and they are willing to pay the price required for success. In the words of Nido Qubein, success is "painful," which means you have to *pay-in-full* for it. Nothing in this life is free.

Amateurs are happy with just doing enough, but they do not have the drive to be the best. They are happy operating at a mediocre level, posing as professionals, and charging people even when they don't get results.

Traitors are people who have to steal to get what they want in life. They may look like amateurs or professionals and have good intentions, but when it comes down to their actions, they become thieves and steal time, money, and resources.

I once wrote down twenty-five people that I regularly spent time with in my personal and professional life. Then I wrote the word *professional, amateur,* or *traitor* next to each name and looked for the patterns and associations in the names.

When I did this, I noticed that while I was running my career as a "pro," I was living my personal life as an "amateur," and I had a graveyard of "traitors" that I tried not to think about.

More interesting is the fact that all of my "pros" were associated and worked together as a team with me in their respective fields.

The "amateurs" were all associated and transacted together. They stuck together, were tightly bonded, and through their daily choices, were committed to mediocrity without even knowing it. I noticed the amateurs in my life had referred amateurs to my business who posed as professionals and later became traitors (this was very alarming).

The "traitors" were all associated with each other and approached me as a group as well. They were a tight-knit group that was like a pack of wolves. It was scary, in hindsight, to see a group of traitors aligned in business and all working together; you can get killed if you find yourself working with a pack of traitors. It cost me dearly to deal with the traitors on my list.

It was revealing to see how my social circles were constructed when measured by this system. The lesson I learned very quickly was that I needed to align myself with the pros, cull the amateurs from my team, and bury the traitors in the past.

Action Step: Please take a moment to do this assessment for yourself. First, write down the 25 people you spend the most time with in your personal and professional life. Next, write the word *professional, amateur,* or *traitor* next to each name and look for the patterns and associations in the names. You may find out something new about who you are transacting with. You will even find out how you are running the different aspects of your life.

PS Don't be afraid to load up the "traitor" category; this is an extremely important category, one I overlooked because I generally do not focus on people who have "screwed" me. This category is in some ways more important than the other two.

Chapter 23

GRIT: THE X FACTOR FOR SUCCESS

For centuries, alchemists searched for the "philosopher's stone," a magical instrument that could turn lead into gold, but they never found it. Every day fools buy lottery tickets hoping to turn "lead into gold."

Explorers searched the globe for centuries looking for the "fountain of youth," only to never find it. Every day people in department stores spend millions of dollars on lotions and potions to cling to their fleeting youth.

Every night audiences in the hundreds of thousands stay up late watching infomercials promising "get rich quick schemes," "get rock hard abs now," and dating programs that claim the man or woman of your dreams is "one phone call away."

We all want success to be easy.

We all want the silver bullet or the magic wand that will make things "easy" and change in an instant.

We all want the secret sauce that will make us an overnight success. These days, it takes ten years to become an "overnight success."

Success is never as easy as it looks!

What if we could increase our probability for success by focusing on one certain personality trait?

There have been hundreds of studies on success, and scientists have found it has nothing to do with intelligence, talent, luck, resources, contacts, or education. However, studies have proven that there is a specific personality trait called "grit" that is directly correlated to success.

Grit is a psychological trait that indicates a person's passion for a particular long-term goal. Grit is associated with perseverance, resilience, ambition, need for achievement, and tenacity.

To make a long explanation short, the grittier a person is, the harder they will fight to succeed.

People with high levels of grit are concerned with winning the marathon, not the sprint. They are long-term thinkers who aim to achieve far-reaching goals and are less concerned with short-term challenges and failures. A person with a high level of grit will move from failure to failure and keep their eyes on the prize.

To quote Winston Churchill, "Success is moving from failure to failure without losing enthusiasm." Churchill understood grit, and he was able to capture the hearts and minds of the British people in World War II. Throughout nearly the entire war, Britain was the underdog, suffering defeat after defeat from the Nazis. However, Churchill was able to inspire his people to become gritty, dig in, and hold on. In the end, the Nazi war machine ran itself into disrepair while the British were able to claim victory by sheer tenacity, despite being the underdog for nearly the entire war.

Many of our parents or grandparents who were who were born in 1920s became extremely gritty due to the fact that at age ten they were in the Great Depression, and by age twenty they were fighting in a world war. If they were strong enough to survive those two events, they came home, built themselves a house with their bare hands, raised four or more children, and worked like slaves until they retired (or died relatively young compared to today's standards).

The World War II generation included a very gritty group of people compared to the baby boomers or the echo boomers. The World War II generation understood that

1) Life is not easy.
2) Persistence wins.
3) Hard work is required for success.
4) Giving up is not an option.
5) Life is not always fun, but keep going.

Today's young people are not conditioned to be gritty like their grandparents or great-grandparents. Today we live in a world of instant text messaging, Facebook, Twitter, video games, instant microwave dinners, and soccer tournaments where the losers are taken out for ice cream.

Gritty people are able to delay gratification, and often this is the number one key to success. Unfortunately, we are conditioned today to want instant gratification, and many of us forget how tough our grandparents were to survive and thrive for the last ninety years.

If you're a success-minded individual, you should focus on becoming more "gritty." To do so

1) Set long-term goals.
2) Train yourself to not be discouraged by failure.
3) Learn to delay gratification.
4) Become passionate about your cause.
5) Never give up.
6) Focus on winning the marathon, not the sprint.
7) Reward yourself for lasting power; do not become a flash in the pan.

Consider one of Aesop's fables, "The Tortoise and the Hare." The hare represents speed. He is flashy; he is loud and proud. But in the end he is the loser. The tortoise, though slow, is persistent, consistent, and gritty. And ultimately wins.

Be the tortoise, not the hare: the future belongs to you.

Chapter 24

HOW TO PROFIT FROM FAILURE: TURN LEMONS INTO LEMONADE

A wise man once said, "When life gives you lemons, make lemonade."

In 2012, I was nominated for Joint Venture Partner of the Year in the Top Investor awards hosted by *Canadian Real Estate Wealth* magazine. Competing in my category were five other very competent investors, all of whom I admire greatly.

I had a fair amount of time to think about the strategic possibilities of my nomination and ran through all of the possible scenarios that such recognition would bring.

My competitors were all very successful investors, and depending on the metrics used to determine a "winner," any one of us could have won the award:

1) The winner could be determined by dollar volume, in which case I would certainly not be the winner. I was not the investor with the biggest deals.

2) The winner could be determined by profits, in which case I would certainly not be the winner. The other investors in the category were working with much larger dollar volumes,

which naturally yielded bigger profits.

3) Or the winner could be determined by story, in which I would have a chance to win.

I had to prepare myself for two scenarios:

1) A scenario in which I win
2) A scenario in which I do not win

It was truly an honor to be nominated alongside such successful investors, and the nomination alone was worth a tremendous amount of value to me.

I thought about the scenario of winning and the scenario of losing for a long time and determined that I would rather lose to a champion than win over an inferior competitor.

In my head, I created a no-lose scenario.

I would either win the award and run with the temporary boost to my brand/marketing or lose and still run with the temporary boost to my brand/marketing. The only way to create a no-lose scenario is by learning to create profit from failure.

I have failed in my life more times than I have succeeded.

They say that the formula for failure is to try to please everyone. In contrast, the formula for success is to take your current rate of failure and double it.

I have doubled my rate of failure many times over and continue to increase my quota. I am not afraid of failing because when life gives me lemons, I have learned how to squeeze out a delicious glass of lemonade.

I have made lemonade so many times in my investing career that I could open up a lemonade stand.

Although I have had many chances to wrestle with failure, many people have not had the luxury of having so many experiences to study and learn from.

The school system conditions us to avoid failure at all costs. In school, we treat failure as seriously as death itself: if you fail, you don't get good grades, and you can't get into a good university, you can't get a good job, and you will starve to death on the street because you have no money.

In many ways, in school, A students learn to associate failure with death. In reality, failure is the essence of life.

We learn our greatest lessons when we fail, and often we use these experiences to craft our identities, our characters, our philosophies, and our stories that make us into champions who can press forward against all odds.

My thinking has changed dramatically over the years when it comes to failure.

I used to get upset when I failed. However, I no longer get upset. When I fail in my current endeavors, I identify and correct my mistake as fast as possible. I then ask myself, *How can I prevent this in the future?* Failing is no longer a negative emotion for me; in fact, I get excited to fail now because it means that I will get an opportunity to learn a lesson. Lessons make me smarter and increase my chances of winning in the future.

FAILURE MANAGEMENT 101

Imagine you're an Olympic athlete for an obscure sport like javelin, in which you take a running start to throw a single spear as far as possible.

You train for ten years, put in more than ten thousand hours of training, forgo sex, good food, alcohol, sleep, professional career opportunities, children, money, and a comfort-filled lifestyle for a chance at competing in the Olympics.

The day of the Olympics comes, and you get one chance, one throw, and in that moment, you will become one of two things:

1) A winner, a medalist, immortalized as a champion in the Olympic Hall of Fame
OR
2) A nobody; you do not qualify, and you miss the distance re-

quired by inches, as your javelin efforts vaporize into thin air.

Your spear falls short of the mark and you do not qualify for a medal.

On Monday morning, when you get back to your home, what do you do when you sit down at the kitchen table and ponder your next move?

Had you achieved success, you would have gotten a sponsorship, a great career opportunity, recognition and fame, etc.

However, you failed. What next?

How do you make lemonade out of the lemons?

How can you create success from the experience?

I have been in situations like this many times. Life is a performance-based sport; you often only get one chance to make something happen, and if you don't, how do you deal with it?

It's not what happens to you in life that matters; it's how you deal with it.

When I was waiting for the speaker at the podium to announce the winner of the Joint Venture Partner of the Year award, I had fully prepared myself for failure.

I desired success, I understood that it was possible, but the final decision was out of my hands—so it was impossible for me to worry.

In hindsight, I was 95 percent prepared for failure and only 5 percent prepared for success.

I was shocked to learn I had won the award, so I obviously did not have a speech ready. I winged a few words at the podium, thanked everyone I could think of, and proceeded with my "success plan" that I had to quickly engineer.

I was so convinced that my larger competitors would win the award that I had given up the idea of success. To avoid disappointment, I had created a plan to deal with failure and was only focused on creating an asset out of failure.

I had become so good at losing and dealing with situations that go wrong that I forgot to plan for situations that go right. Getting good at losing, however, is one of the major pillars of success. It helps us take risks and allows us to win—even when we lose. Life becomes very easy when we can find ways to win from failure, especially when we learn to monetize these situations.

When I think about the Joint Venture Partner of the Year award I won, I am convinced my story is what captured the judges' imaginations. I did not have the biggest deal, the biggest profit, the highest dollar volumes, or the sexiest deal. However, what I *did* have was a great "rags to riches" story that explains my investment career. My story for 2012 begins with failure and ends with success.

Most people give up when they fail; I have learned to push through failures until I can turn them into successes.

In your own life, learn to spot the "good" in the "bad" and package it into a marketable asset you can use to your advantage.

Failure is a necessary ingredient to success, and many people don't understand that success comes in cycles and is more like a wheel than a defined destination.

Picture the Ferris wheel at the local fair. When you are at the top of the wheel (success), the only way to get back to the top (success) is to go through the bottom (failure). Life is much like a Ferris wheel: to get the top, we must rotate through the cycles at the bottom.

In the words of Napoleon Hill, "Every adversity, every failure, every heartache carries with it the seed on an equal or greater benefit."

Learn to find these seeds, then plant them, water them, and watch them grow.

"Jack and the Beanstalk" is one of my favorite stories, one that perfectly describes my life so far.
    1) Jack trades his mother's cow for some "magic beans."
    2) Jack brings the beans home to mother, who curses him and throws them out the window to spite him.

3) The next morning, a huge beanstalk has grown into the clouds and Jack decides to climb up the beanstalk.
4) Jack finds a castle in the clouds that is ruled by a giant.
5) Jack slays the giant.
6) Jack climbs down the beanstalk with the princess (his life partner), the golden harp (his calling), and the golden goose (his ability to make money).
7) Jack began his journey as a boy and became a man through the process.

Although Jack is successful in the story, he begins with failure. He traded his mother's last milk-producing cow for three magic beans. The beans have no intrinsic value, and his mother believes he has made a bad trade; in her anger, she throws the beans out the window. After the beanstalk grows from the magic beans, Jack climbs into the clouds, goes through a series of trials, and becomes a successful man.

My investing career has been the same way, and my first two years in the business were a series of rather tough trials that could have easily become fatal failures. However, through persistence and tenacity, I have always found ways to turn failures into successes. Every time I have failed or experienced a setback, I have been successful in converting failures into greater successes and have become consistent in my results.

The next time you fail, look for the opportunity to create an equal or greater success.

I have become better and better at this skill each time I practice it. In my lifetime, I aim to become a master of "failing" so I will constantly be in a "no-lose" situation. Life truly is a "no-lose" game if we approach it with the right attitude and the right level of creativity.

"Empty your mind, be formless, shapeless—like water. Now you put water into a cup, it becomes the cup, you put water into a bottle, it becomes the bottle, you put it in a teapot, it becomes the teapot. Now water can flow or it can crash. Be water, my friend." —Bruce Lee

Part 3

THE EXECUTION: THE ART OF DEAL MAKING

This section focuses on the art of deal making and the "hows" of real estate. I will also cover the principles of making money in real estate and the broad concepts that must be grasped to pursue the fastest way to wealth.

Chapter 25

THE LAW OF CERTAINTY AND THE TWENTY-ONE STEPS TO A JV DEAL

Some people believe in luck; I believe in the law of certainty: certain things done in a certain way will achieve certain results certainly! In order to raise money for a real estate joint venture, the game must be played in a certain way. If the game is played in a certain order, then certain results are certain to occur. If the game is played out of order, the chances for putting the money, the people, and the deal together become slim.

The following is a list of twenty-one steps that I use to put the Money, the People, and the Deal together in a sustainable way:

1) Determine your "why." Why are you in business? Why do you need to succeed?

2) Pick five people to be on your "to be" list. These people can be heroes, mentors, or coaches. You want to keep a list of people to study so you have vision in your business and in your life.

3) Create your vision and find your dream. Real estate is full of setbacks; without a clear vision and dream, you will stop at the first sign of resistance. Create a vision plan with a spe-

cific dream that you wish to achieve. This will motivate you through the ups and downs of real estate and will help you to inspire and magnetize others toward you.

4) Raise your credit. Call every credit card company that is available in your local area and increase your credit limit, or apply for credit before starting your venture. Real estate is a game that requires large amounts of credit; you will be happy to have a large amount of credit once you get started.

5) Build a team. Building a team is an ongoing process. At first you will assemble a team of the best people you can find; as you gain experience, your team will get better and better. Initially you will want a mortgage broker, a lawyer, an accountant, a Realtor®, a contractor, and perhaps a property manager.

6) Build your joint venture proposal money-raising binder. This is your business plan and will be a very important tool for raising money from investors. Spend some time on this proposal; organization and preparation can outperform experience in this area.

7) Look at one hundred deals; analyze one hundred deals. Do the numbers on paper for one hundred deals to create a paper track record. If you don't have a track record yet, this step is very important because it allows you to gain experience in your market without investing any money. You will learn the prices of the different areas and what seems to sell and what does not. Get your Realtor® to help you with the numbers if you are missing data.

8) Analyze your social network to determine the people who are your warm market and would be happy to talk to you about investing in real estate. Also determine your cold market or the people who would not be expecting a call from you. Make a list of all the people you know, and estimate the dollar amount that they would be willing to invest. Don't stop the list until you have one million dollars of potential capital.

9) Distribute articles about real estate through your social media to brand yourself as a real estate expert to your cold market. Begin contacting your warm market to gauge their interest in

investing in real estate.

10) Build a potential investor list; get permission to contact these investors when you have a deal that is ready to go.

11) Begin writing offers and get a deal under contract. Make sure you have a due diligence period and an escape clause in the case you cannot find an investor in time.

12) Shop your deal to your interested investors; sit down with them face-to-face, open your binder, and show them how they make money and when the deal will return their capital.

13) Get two investors interested in the deal and one committed to close the deal.

14) Get a joint venture agreement made between you and your money partner, and get the agreement signed.

15) Obtain financing for your deal through your mortgage broker.

16) Begin marketing the property for viability. If there is insufficient interest, or if you are having second thoughts, you can drop the deal.

17) Close on the deal; take the title.

18) Acquire the property, fix any loose ends, then prepare to renovate or to rent out the property.

19) Fill the suite or renovate depending on the strategy.

20) Manage the project and ensure success.

21) Manage ongoing investor relations and get referrals.

Action Step: Review the twenty-one steps to a joint venture deal, identify which steps will be a challenge for you, and find a coach or mentor to help you through the process. (Coaching programs are offered at MoneyPeopleDeal.com.)

Chapter 26

WHY THE BEST DEALS ARE CREATED AND CANNOT BE BOUGHT

A lmost every day I get asked by one person or another, "How do you find great deals?" I often hear people complain all across North America, "You can't do that here," or "There aren't any deals where I live."

The truth is that deals are everywhere, if you are trained to see them. At the time of this writing, Canadian real estate was at an all-time high, and I was making all of my money in Canada. The US was at an all-time low, and there were lots of opportunities in the US as well. However, when the market is high, we use one set of strategies; when the market is low, we use another set of strategies. To a skilled investor it doesn't matter if the market is up or down in real estate; there is always money to be made. The opportunities change, but the truth remains: deals are made—not found!

When someone asks me, "How do I find a great deal?" My answers are always vague:

1) Deals come from ads I put up.
2) They come from my network of professionals (fellow investors, lawyers, property managers, etc.).
3) They come from bird dogs or wholesalers.
4) They come from inside connections with centers of influence.

5) Deals come from my blog.

6) Or they come from one of my Realtors®.

Every week I look at more than a dozen deals and send out between five and twenty-five offers. I keep very active and can often get great discounts or no-money-down deals that are not offered to the general public. Finding great deals is a numbers game and a contact sport. The more contacts you make, the higher your numbers are for actions, the better deals you will get.

A great ratio to follow is the 100:10:3:1 rule, which states, "Look at one hundred deals on paper. Write offers on ten desirable properties. Three offers will be accepted. One offer will be acceptable."

Keep the numbers high, look at lots of properties, and profits or no-money deals will be found every time.

However ...

Just because a deal is no money down or at a "discount" doesn't mean it's a good deal.

The truth with deals, whether in real estate or business, is that they are often cherry-picked before you get access to them, and the best ones are usually taken. Even a private deal goes through at least a dozen sets of eyes before it gets to you.

If a deal is so great, then why hasn't anyone bought it yet?

The answer to the question is there is no such thing as a good deal, because the best deals are created, not bought.

The formula for a great deal is simple:

1) Find a great opportunity.

2) Add value.

3) Collect profit.

The key with this formula is step two. Adding value is the hardest part of this cycle, and figuring out how to maximize the opportunity takes the most skill.

I would estimate that the average person gets eight great opportunities every day (real estate or just personal life opportunities). However, it takes a certain pair of eyes to recognize the eight opportunities that fall into our laps and a very sharp skill set to add value and collect profit.

At this stage of my career, I have deals coming to me daily, and the biggest challenge is figuring out which deals to pursue and which ones to drop.

When evaluating deals, I ask myself, *Which opportunity can I force the most value out of? Which deals take too much time or effort? Which deals can be done the fastest? Which deals will align with my mission in the best way?*

Often I have found that the more creative I can get with a deal, the higher my profits go. However, just because I get creative doesn't mean I'm ensured a profit.

There are many times when creativity doesn't work; we have to be very careful and give creative approaches a sober second look.

The questions I always ask when someone approaches me with a deal are

1) Why is this a good deal?

> a. Is it short term, medium, or long term?
> b. Is there equity built in to the deal?
> c. Does it have cash flow?
> d. Can I use multiple strategies on this deal?

2) What is everyone else failing to see?

> a. Is this property mismarketed? Can I remarket it differently for profit?
> b. Is there excess land I can subdivide?
> c. Can I remove a wall to change the floor plan?
> d. Can utilities be split to increase profits on a multiunit deal?
> e. Can I change the number of bedrooms/bathrooms to make the property sell faster?
> f. Would the property benefit from a finished basement, a deck, or a garage?

3) What mistakes did the vendor/seller make?

a. Was the vendor asking too much for the property, and has it now sat on the market too long as a result?

b. Did they market the property dirty and cluttered?

c. Does the property smell bad, deterring buyers from purchasing it?

d. Did they market the property with tenants in it? Or without tenants in it? Either can be beneficial or detrimental to the sale of property.

4) What is my unfair advantage with this deal?

a. Do I have inside information on the area or developments happening in the area?

b. Do I have experience owning/operating this type of asset?

c. Can I operate this property more efficiently than the previous owners?

5) How can I maximize my profits?

a. Can I create profits through aesthetics and design?

b. Historically, what is the highest sale price for a comparable property like this in the area?

c. What are buyers looking for in this area?

6) How fast can this deal be done?

a. Can this deal be done in ninety days or less?

b. Is this a desirable area where I can sell or fill a suite quickly?

c. Are there any factors that can slow this deal down?

7) What is the effort required on my part?

a. How much of my time will this deal take?

b. How much management skill will this deal require?

c. How much marketing skill will it require?

d. How much capital needs to be raised?

e. How quickly does the capital need to be raised?

8) How safe is my partner's capital?

a. Is this property liquid? Can I sell it quickly?

b. What factors contribute to the value of this property?

c. Is there a chance that this property loses value while I own it?

9) What threatens my position on this deal?

    a. What external threats can compromise my position in owning this piece of property?

    b. Is the area changing?

    c. Is new development happening nearby that would be direct competition?

10) Can I negotiate further on the price/terms?

    a. Does the vendor have further room to move on the price?

    b. Is the vendor open to doing a terms deal?

    c. If I drop the deal and come back later, can I get a better price/terms?

11) How can I get creative with this deal and make it even more valuable to me?

    a. Can this deal be used for branding?

    b. Are there advertising opportunities with the property (billboards/signage)?

    c. Are there parking/storage opportunities?

12) Can I repurpose this deal and sell it to another audience (rezone, repurpose, assembly, commercial/residential)?

    a. Is this property most valuable in its current state?

    b. Can it be rezoned for profit?

    c. Is it better as a rental? Or a residential resale?

The wonderful thing about real estate is that there is a very high degree of control. A real estate entrepreneur controls just about every aspect of a deal, and value can be created in an infinite number of ways.

I was at a real estate trade show earlier this year, and I looked at forty different real estate companies who were promoting their products and their deal inventory. I was very impressed with the creative and innovative ways that the forty different companies were able to find unique ways to create deals, create value, and in turn, create profit.

The ability to create a deal is an entrepreneurial skill that very few people are good at. When I think of a person who can create a deal, I think of

Donald Trump. If you study Trump, you will find that almost every one of his deals is created, engineered, and innovative. Every deal is different, and he can see value where no one else can.

One deal that comes to mind is 40 Wall Street, which Trump bought for $1 million and is now worth close to $400 million. Some people say it's the best real estate deal of all time.

Most real estate entrepreneurs make amazing returns when they double the value of a property. Through creativity and deal engineering, Trump was able to increase the value of the property by four-hundredfold.

What deal can you multiply the value by four hundred? I lack the skills to create a deal like that yet, and very few people in the world have a skill set like Trump. That's why he's a billionaire and most people aren't.

When analyzing a potential deal, think of the ways you can "create" a great deal where most people fail to see a profit. The best deals of all are missed opportunities that are often obscure and mismarketed. Get a mismarketed opportunity, create value, and reap the rewards. The formula is simple.

Action Step: Look at one hundred deals on paper, find the most profitable opportunities, and make ten offers. Can you spot the profit that others aren't seeing?

Chapter 27

BUY RATIONAL, SELL IRRATIONAL

B eauty is in the eye of the beholder, and so is value.

Every day, we, the human race, wake up and chase value until we drop dead from exhaustion at night. It doesn't matter if you are Donald Trump sitting on a multibillion-dollar real estate portfolio or a monk in a temple. We are all chasing value.

The real question is, What is value and what is valuable?

Of course, value is highly subjective and can be very hard to determine.

I always find it fascinating to see how excited people are to buy new clothes. Shopping malls are filled with rabid people who are frantically purchasing new garments to wear, and six months later the clothes that they purchased will be donated to charity or thrown away.

The value of the clothes goes from *I will sacrifice my financial health to wear this* to *I will never wear this piece of garbage again.*

The same thing happens with electronics. The day that Apple releases a new iPhone or iPod, people are camping out overnight to get their hands on the new gadget and will pay a mortgage payment to own it. Six months later, the same people are giving the old iPhone to their dog or are using it as a coaster on a coffee table because the newer, thinner model came out.

But what about investments? Real estate? Houses?

What is the true intrinsic value of a house?

Most middle-class people will say, *Our house is our biggest asset!* They will have nearly all of their net worth tied up in their home.

But what is the house actually worth? What is any house actually worth?

The truth is, all real estate is actually worth zero dollars. Land and buildings are completely worthless.

If you would like to see the true value of land and buildings, drive to Detroit, where you can buy a city block for $1 and no one wants to buy. People who live in Detroit would rather have a $1 taco at Taco Bell than own the liability of a city block.

Land, real estate, houses, and buildings only get value when there is a use for them and an end user. The end user places their subjective value on the real estate, and that is where values come from.

There are more people who want to live in Manhattan than Detroit. That's why Manhattan real estate is worth so much more than properties in Detroit. At the end of the day, real estate is only worth what the end user is willing to pay. However, one metric I have been using more and more of lately is dollars per square foot.

When comparing two similar properties, dollars per square foot is one of the best ways to measure the current and future value of the property. For example, in 2013 many desirable houses in Winnipeg traded in the $200 to $250 per square foot range. If you can make a purchase at $100 per square foot in an area that is trading at $200 to $250, you have an opportunity for profit.

Construction in Winnipeg for a new build with land is approximately $140 to $200 per square foot, so if you can purchase for less than $140 to $200, you are getting the house for cheaper than it would be to build.

Likewise, if you pay $300 per square foot, you are paying more than it costs to build.

When analyzing retail single-family homes, dollars per square foot is an excellent metric for intrinsic value of property.

BUY ON INTRINSIC VALUE; SELL ON EMOTIONAL VALUE

One of the easiest ways to profit in any market is to

1) Buy on intrinsic value and
2) Sell on emotional value

There is always profit in markets that have irrational buyers. Irrational buyers bring irrational amounts of money into a market to make irrational purchases.

For example, the neighborhood River Heights in Winnipeg is a desirable neighborhood where people will pay irrational amounts of money to get their kids into the local schools. In River Heights properties trade for $200 to $300 per square foot, prices that are well above cost to build.

However, in up-and-coming parts of town, there are "rational" buyers who will only pay prices that are less than construction prices. These areas will trade at $100 to $180 dollars per square foot.

The key for profit is to buy with an intrinsic value, pump the value, and sell to an emotional, irrational buyer. Irrational buyers are unconcerned with they're actually paying. They want the product and perceive that they need it. If you have a business, you want irrational buyers—consumers who allow you to create massive spreads in your products and grow your business.

Do what you can to attract irrational buyers. When you capture these buyers, take great care of them, and they will take great care of you.

Action Step: Name three retail stores where consumers pay irrational prices for retail items. These stores can be clothing, electronics, home furnishings, or cosmetics. Now think of three wholesale or non-retail stores where consumers pay rational prices for goods. Think of groceries, outlet malls, auctions, or liquidation centers. Note the differences in the buying experience. Which store do you prefer to shop at?

Chapter 28

FUNDAMENTAL INVESTING VS. TECHNICAL TRADING AND CASH VS. CASH FLOW

In investing, there are two major schools of thought: fundamental investors and technical traders.

In real estate investing, the best example of a fundamental investor would be someone who does long-term buy-and-hold properties. These investors are looking at the market on a macro level and rely on the underlying fundamentals of the market rather than the technical price of the asset.

A technical trader is someone who "flips" properties. These investors are generally trading properties that they hold for no longer than six months at most. They buy, force appreciation, and sell in a short period of time. These traders are more focused on the buy-and-sell prices of a specific asset than the underlying market fundamentals.

Both strategies can be successful, and both can make a lot of money. In the end, fundamental and technical strategies should be used together to create cash both immediately and in the future.

The most important thing about choosing a strategy is that we understand the pros and cons of fundamentals and technicals. We need to know how to find value in each strategy and know which strategy to use in a given market.

In real estate investing, a fundamental investor will look at market fundamentals such as:

1) **Industry**: Industry is important because real estate is only valuable when there are jobs around to pay for it. This is why a city block in Detroit can sell for $1 and a single apartment unit in Manhattan sells for $20 million. Detroit has a troubled economy because the local industries have disappeared, and so have the jobs. Manhattan, on the other hand, has an abundance of major industries and high-paying jobs that drive the obscene prices that Manhattan commands. Jobs and industry are two of the most important fundamentals of real estate.

2) **Net Migration**: Are more people moving into a geographic area or are they moving out? If more people are moving in, demand goes up and prices will rise. In markets where oil is discovered, real estate skyrockets because of all the new people that move in to take on the new jobs. Western Canada is littered with oil towns that have steady, positive net migration because of the "black gold rush." On the flip side, if you own real estate in a mining town where the mine goes out of business, be prepared for a real estate crash because the net migration will become negative fast. Pay close attention to what is happening in your market and know how many people are moving in or out every year.

3) **Transportation**: Is the market we are considering accessible or not? Can you transport goods in and out of the market? Northern Canada is filled with worthless real estate because there has been no transportation established far up north. If people cannot easily move to and from the piece of property, chances are it's worthless. An easy strategy to deploy when selecting a market is to follow new trade routes, highways, or flight paths of airlines. Where transportation goes, so do jobs and net migration. Pay attention to new transportation routes; where transportation goes, so do profits.

Investors who play a fundamental game have the benefit of slow-moving markets and can make educated choices based on slow and steady research. Over time, if chosen correctly, fundamentals can make create large profits with very little work. When I do buy and holds, I always pay very close attention to the fundamentals to make sure that I am parking my money in the most efficient way possible.

Technical investors are very different from fundamental investors. Fundamental investors are concerned with

1) Short-term technical movements in the market
2) Specific entry and exit prices of the market
3) Specific, short time frames

Technical traders do not really invest in a market; they trade in a market. When I flip houses, I think like a technical trader: I look for a distressed or undervalued asset, force appreciation, and make a calculated and speedy exit.

Since the positions are short in technical trading, I don't have to worry as much about industry, net migration, and transportation that move slowly over months and years. All that matters is the entry price, exit price, and that the market holds while I own the asset. Since real estate is a slow game, especially in my market (Winnipeg), I usually don't have to worry about a sudden downturn in the market.

What is more important in flipping houses is making sure that the end user (the customer) desires to purchase my product and that they can afford it. Many flippers/traders get stuck because they flip in areas with no demand or areas where the end user does not want to live. Pay very close attention to the customers, specifically the customers with money. Always give the people what they want.

Doing short-term real estate trades or flipping is a retail business where the buyers buy on aesthetics and emotion. Give your customers a beautiful product that they deeply desire, make sure your margins are high, and sell fast! Flipping houses is retail and exactly the same as running a retail clothing store, a retail furniture store, or a retail furnishing store. Create a beautiful spectacle, dazzle the customer with retail lighting, pump up the emotions, and create excitement. Staging sells, beauty sells, shiny kitchens sell, lifestyle sells, and emotions sell.

In my career I have switched many times from a "cash flow" (fundamental) strategy to a "cash" (technical) strategy. Depending on the needs of my business, I will switch strategies as required so I take advantage of opportunities as I find them.

If I were to start over in real estate, I would start with a "cash" strategy and convert to "cash flow" over time. The beauty with real estate is that there is something for everyone, and the more creative you get with a strategy (generally), the more money you can make.

Action Step: Consider the requirements for a fundamental buy-and-hold strategy vs. a technical buy-and-sell strategy. Which one is better suited to your market, your financial situation, and your personality? Begin assembling your team, and consider the different team you would need to deploy each strategy.

Chapter 29

WHY MORONS GET RICH AND GENIUSES DIE BROKE:
THE SIX PROFIT CENTERS OF REAL ESTATE

Real estate is one of the only industries I can think of where investors or owner/operators can be absolute morons and still win.

Every day I see scores of smart broke people who can barely make a living in jobs and businesses that they spent five to fifteen years of educating themselves for. It makes no sense to see these people commit such large portions of their lives just be broke and barely scraping by. The saddest part is that most of these people are highly intelligent A students who never really learned about money. I learned this firsthand when I spent four years in university to earn a degree that qualified me for a ten-dollar-per-hour office job in the middle of the night. Times are changing; it doesn't necessarily pay to be smart anymore.

On the flip side, as a full-time real estate investor, I often see investors in the market who are total morons—people who can still make impressive profits or break even on bad deals that they completely screwed up on and shouldn't have done in the first place.

Why do so many smart, educated A students with high-priced educations struggle to make a living while total morons can win big profits in real estate?

The answer to that question, I believe, has to do more with the industry and "profit centers" than it does with business acumen, skills, education, brains, or experience.

For example, I know of an investor in my market who decided to buy a commercial condo for $80,000. He planned to rezone it to residential by adding a kitchen sink (it already had a bedroom and full bath and was missing a kitchen sink). After adding a sink, he calculated that he would be able to sell the condo for more than $160,000.

When my friend applied to the city for rezoning, they made him gut the apartment, bring it up to code, fix the broken roof trusses of the condo building, and then he had to refinish the entire condo. He also had to add soundproofing, fireproofing, update the ducts and venting, and increase the standards of just about everything in the condo.

The process took twenty-four months because he was inexperienced with renovations management and the rezoning/development process.

After twenty-four months of financial bleeding, my friend still had an opportunity to break even or make a small profit because, during his renovation period, another developer decided to build brand-new condos next door priced at $300,000 to $500,000.

This new information can increase the exit price of my friend's condo and may help him turn a profit. There is no other industry I can think of where an entrepreneur can fail on every single part of a business and still turn a profit or break even. The market will eventually bail out the morons every time if they wait long enough. The question is, How long do you have to wait until you get bailed out?

Now back to the real question: Why can a moron in real estate beat a genius in another industry?

The answer, I believe, is that real estate has six natural profit centers. In other words, a real estate deal naturally makes money in six ways, while most businesses or people with jobs make money in one way.

Take a lemonade stand, for example. A lemonade stand only makes money when it sells a glass of lemonade. This business has one profit center; it can only earn money when it sells a glass of lemonade.

Then consider a car dealership. It has multiple profit centers. It can make money when a car is bought, sold, financed, leased, traded in, warrantied, rustproofed, or serviced. The dealership also makes money on the car's oil changes, air filters, tires, periodic checkups, spare parts, collision repair, painting/repainting, etc.

The amount of profit centers that a car dealership can draw revenue from is at least over ten. This is why car companies can grow so large; there are so many profit centers, many of which are residual—this makes for a good business.

I would rather own a car dealership with over ten profit centers than have one profit center at a lemonade stand.

The fact of the matter is that many "smart" people only have one profit center: They trade time for money. If they want more money, they can trade more time; there are no other options. It doesn't matter if you are a doctor, lawyer, or janitor. Anyone with a job trades time for money.

If these "smart" people cannot find a buyer for their time (a.k.a. employer), then their revenues and profits go to zero. To me, this is an extremely risky strategy. I find it scary that most people think that this is "security." One profit center is not a sound financial strategy.

On the other side of the coin, the car dealership we looked at above has at least ten ways to make money. If a customer comes into the dealership, they can sell them ten or more products and services. If a car is sold, there are residual sales for the company and the dealership makes even more cash. The customers have to come back to the dealership to maintain their cars, and while the customers come back for service, they will try to sell them a new car.

When you look at the amount of profit centers that a car dealership has, it's no wonder that the manufacturing of automobiles drove the industrial revolution—there are mountains of money to be made off these inefficient machines.

But why can morons win in real estate? There are six major profit centers in real estate, and the best part is that most of these profit centers are passive and easy to manage. Geniuses with university degrees and high-paying jobs make profit in one way; morons with real estate make money in six ways.

THE SIX PROFIT CENTERS OF REAL ESTATE

1) **Cash Flow:** Cash flow is the most important profit center in real estate. On a buy and hold, cash flow is king! Cash flow drives the entire business of real estate and is often the reason why people want to enter or exit the game of real estate. Most people get into the business for the passive income and cash flow. Ironically, most people get out of the business because of the passive income and cash flow. They either get out because they retire and are successful, or they cannot manage the cash flow and have to sell all of their assets. Either way, cash flow drives more people in and out of real estate than anything else. Although cash flow is always alluring and exciting, it is not the biggest moneymaker on most deals. The actual monthly residual profits are merely a bonus on most deals and cannot compare to the other profit centers associated with real estate.

2) **Instant Equity:** Instant equity is extremely important to me when I make a real estate purchase. I always want to make profit on day one by buying an undervalued asset. Everyone loves to get a deal when we buy something, and I want to make money immediately on day one. Investors who buy on the retail market off MLS can get pressured by Realtors® to buy at market prices. You either have to have a very good Realtor® on your team to negotiate a good deal or buy privately to get a good amount of equity in a purchase. Equity on day one usually comes from mismarketed properties that either don't have enough exposure to buyers or are exposed to the wrong types of buyers. Either way, instant equity is one of my favorite ways to make money.

3) **Leverage**: One of the main reasons why I choose to invest in real estate is the leverage. For every dollar I put in to real estate, the bank will invest with me (usually between three to five times of what you I put in).

Leverage allows my returns to explode and jump to double-digit levels because I am investing with bank money and not my own. In real estate, $10,000 will buy you $100,000 of property. In stocks, $10,000 will get you $10,000 of stock. Banks will not lend on their own stock because they see stocks as risky (even their own). I find it disturbing to consider that banks will lend you money for real estate every day of the week, but will not give you a loan to purchase their own stock. If the bank is willing to put their money into real estate, so should you.

4) **Appreciation**: Appreciation is a wonderful "bonus" that professional real estate investors look for in a deal. Many novices don't understand appreciation and think all countries and cities appreciate together in sync. However, in reality, real estate is broken down into markets, submarkets, and specific city blocks. What I look for in deals are undervalued submarkets or city blocks that are appreciating. I am an advocate of fundamentals and like to stack the odds in my favor.

What controls appreciation? Mostly supply and demand; however, the physical condition of the actual property can be manipulated to force appreciation. One of my favorite strategies is to purchase run-down or nonfunctional properties for a discount and force appreciation by fixing the problem properties.

Economy is a huge driver of appreciation, and economies are broken down into markets and submarkets. You always have to ask yourself, *How is the money moving in or out of this market?*

When economies are booming in a city or a town, people start to move into town. When economies are threatened, people are usually start moving out of town to look for better opportunities.

High interest rates can make properties more or less affordable and keep money in or out of a market. This can stop the liquidity of properties and make them very hard to actualize appreciation. Pay attention to interest rates. In 2013, interest rates were at an all-time low, but in the next ten years, they will rise because they can't stay low forever.

5) **Depreciation**: Depreciation is an accounting technique that amortizes the property over twenty-five years, or the life of the building. An accountant can create paper losses and shelter revenues from taxes by creating paper losses.

Recapture: However, there is always a downside; recapture is when the government wants all of their tax savings back when you decide to sell the building. If you are going to depreciate your buildings, consider the cost and benefit of this technique.

Why depreciate? A dollar today is worth more than a dollar ten years from now. Money is always becoming less valuable every day. Get your money out of your real estate as fast as possible to get it moving as fast as possible. Money is a currency and must move to be valuable.

6) **Principal Paydown:** I always grin when I look at my principal pay-down on my mortgages. I used to be scared of having high-balance mortgages on my properties because I could only see the liability of the debt. Now when I see a high-balance mortgage, I see a large amount of equity being built every year.

Consider this: If you have a thirty-year mortgage of $1,000,000, in thirty years that mortgage will be paid off, and you will have made $1,000,000 in equity. This is one of the most powerful profit centers in real estate. The more mortgage debt you have, the more equity you make every month. If your properties are managed properly and cash flowing, this can be a huge moneymaker over time.

What's even better about principal paydown is that this equity can be taken out tax-free through a debt refinance. If the property is re-financed with a new mortgage, the equity gains that you made on the principal paydown are given to you tax free because the gains are not earnings—they are considered a loan instead, and the government cannot take taxes on a loan.

Action Step: It's always easier to be on the outside of the market wishing you were in than to be on the inside wishing you were out. So the next time you consider doing a real estate deal, ask yourself, *How will I make money through the six profit centers? If everything goes wrong, how am I protected from loss? How does this deal align with my goals?*

Chapter 30

WHAT RECESSION?
HOW TO BECOME
RECESSION-PROOF

There is a moment in my life I will never forget: I was watching 50 Cent, the famous rapper, on a television interview. He was wearing a suit and dressed like a businessman—not like a rapper or a drug dealer, contrary to his public image. The interviewer was marveling at 50 Cent's business acumen and his successes outside of music. There are two parts of the interview that will stay with me forever:

1) 50 Cent made a huge profit selling Vitamin Water. From what I understood in the interview, he was a venture capitalist on the deal and sold the company for around $300 million to Coca-Cola. He chose Vitamin Water because it had the same markup as crack cocaine (his first business as a child).

2) When the interviewer asked about the economic recession, 50 Cent replied, "Recession? What recession? Where I come from, there is always a recession . . . The recession is a middle-class problem, not one for the rich or the poor."

When 50 Cent said those words, they had a striking effect on me that changed the way I thought about business. I had always intuitively felt there were only two places to be in the market if you want to be successful and sustainable.

1) Be at the top, the luxury level, and have the highest margins.
2) Be at the bottom, have the lowest price, and win on volume.

Any market has an assortment of prices, values, and products. What I look for as an entrepreneur is market pressure. I want to know where the pressure points are in the market.

For example, Winnipeg has a shortage of rental units. The local government, through strict regulations on rental units, artificially caused the shortage of rental units. The tight government regulations drove outside developers and investors to take their money and invest in other cities. Consequently, there are roughly five hundred vacant rental units in the whole city with a population of over seven hundred thousand people. The average household income is slightly lower than other cities, and the purchasing power is usually around $30,000 to $50,000 per person for most renters.

This means that if you have a rental unit under $1,000, you will have a lineup of people applying to rent it because there are far too many people at bottom of the market. These people have no purchasing power and are fighting to get in. There are limited options at the bottom and it's easy to make a sale.

This same principle is why slumlords make so much money. Slumlords set their rents so low that there is always a lineup of impoverished renters willing to rent their suites. The slumlords never have to repair anything because they know they will always have customers. Their customers are on social assistance or other forms of welfare, and the revenue comes directly from the government, who is the most stable customer around.

Slumlords are at the bottom of the market, where there is no such thing as a recession. Slumlords are at one of the most stable pressure points in the market because they service the bottom only. The bottom always has lots of customers because many customers have no money, are cheap, or just want the basic, bare-minimum product. Other examples of recession-proof, "bottom-market" businesses are McDonald's and Walmart. Many customers only go to those two establishments because of the price.

In contrast to the bottom of the market is the top of the market. The top of the market is often called "luxury" and reserved for those who can pay a premium price for a premium product. Donald Trump, when he built Trump Tower decades ago, chose to build the most luxurious, amazing apartments in Manhattan. These units were so stunning that the wealthiest luxury clients in the world would pay premiums just to live in the iconic Trump Tower. In real estate, Donald Trump caters to the global elite who will pay a premium for goods and services, as long as they have the best in the world. For entrepreneurs who sell to the top of the market, money is not an issue for their customers because luxury clients will pay any price just to have the best.

In 2008, when I worked at an Internet company that sold luxury hotel rooms, we would always have middle-class tire-kickers phoning in, "trying to get a bargain because there was a recession." I had to remind these people daily that "in luxury products, there is never a recession and that modest discounts are rare." Customers will pay full price because they want the best. When you are at the top in the market, there is no recession. Luxury clients will always pay premiums to have the best; money is never an issue when quality and value are the best in the world.

But between the top of the market and the bottom of the market is "no man's land," also known as the middle of the market. (I absolutely hate being in the middle of the market because this is where recessions destroy businesses and entrepreneurs.)

Consumers at the middle of the market are usually middle-class people who have jobs as well as monthly bills, credit card debts, car loans, and mortgages to pay. They also want piano lessons, hockey, and ballet for the kids; plus a once-a-year vacation; savings for retirement; and rainy-day funds—and still expect to eat out three to five times a week.

These people are usually loaded down with so much debt and liability that they are walking a tight rope. If they make a mistake in their budget or lose $100 to an emergency, they suddenly have to cancel their vacation to Mexico ...

If you're the Mexican hoping to sell the vacation to your middle-class friend, you're out of luck and have just lost a price-sensitive customer who can no longer afford your product.

Middle-market people are extremely price sensitive. Every single sway in the economy shakes them, and they drop like flies when things get really bad.

What's worse about selling to middle customers is that they have enough purchasing power to be choosey, but not enough to be luxury. It's hard to determine what they want, and they are mobile enough to be fickle with you and your product. If someone offers them a better bargain, they will be gone to save a few dollars.

There is loyalty at the top, as long as you are the best.

There is loyalty at the bottom, as long as you are the cheapest.

There is no loyalty in the middle market; it is a savage place to be.

Whenever I look at a business, design one, or analyze one, I always want it to be at the top or the bottom of the market. The middle is the scariest place to be.

Recessions can wipe out the middle in a heartbeat, especially with the middle class becoming an endangered species. If your customers are wiped out, so are you.

It's my policy to avoid marketing to the middle, because that is where all the problems are for two reasons:

1) They have enough purchasing power to have options and avoid the bottom.
2) They do not have enough purchasing power to have luxury at the top

They float between the top and the bottom and land wherever they feel like.

The top of the market operates on the emotion of want. The bottom of the market operates on the emotion of need.

I always want my customer to either need or want me. In the middle, your clients neither need nor want you, and this is a huge threat to your business.

In my mind, there is no such thing as a recession because I always focus on the top or the bottom of the market and let other people take the risk of the middle.

Although I may look like a "risk-taking" entrepreneur, I am actually extremely risk averse and like to bet on "sure things." By focusing on the right pressure points in the market and executing your businesses properly with attention to detail, there is no reason why your business cannot become recession-proof.

Action Step: Where do you usually choose to play in the market? Do you prefer to be at the top, bottom, or middle?

Chapter 31

SPEED: WHY FAST WINS AND SLOW LOSES IN THE MARKET

Speed is a virtue that has been coveted throughout the ages.

In the jungle, animals with speed would dominate the terrain over bigger, slower animals. In evolution, animals that developed to be large with heavy armor always lost the evolutionary race to animals that were lighter and faster with sharp teeth and claws.

In warfare, throughout the ages, the faster, more mobile armies were always able to wipe out slower, heavily armored forces—whether we are referring to Attila the Hun, with his mounted archers vs. the slow, heavily armored Roman Legion, or Hitler in World War II, with his Blitzkrieg forces that dominated the sedentary French and Polish troops.

Speed is a virtue in all arenas and is a key to victory.

Today in technology, companies that can embrace change and implement with great speed are the ones that survive. In the past, companies like Apple were able to innovate with products like the iPod and take the market by surprise. Apple had the advantage and implemented new ideas before any of the competitors could react. The advantage of speed allowed Apple to take over and dominate a market long before a competitor could think of stepping in.

Think of iPods . . . Small children call every single music player an iPod. A little girl will point to an analogue record player and say, *Look Daddy, that's a big iPod!* That is the power of speed.

In real estate investing, or investing in general, speed (in my opinion) makes the difference between a novice, intermediate, and advanced investor.

One night a friend of mine and I were talking about our goals for the upcoming year. Every real estate investor, regardless of skill level, always wants to add more transactions and doors to their portfolio. I mentioned to my friend that I was setting the goal of doing one hundred transactions that year.

This was way out of my friend's frame of reference; he couldn't comprehend that kind of volume or speed. He asked me how many transactions I completed that year (twelve to sixteen by the end of the year was my estimate). He was impressed with my ambition and wanted to know how I was going to have an 800 percent increase in my business.

The answer is speed; some experts would say the "velocity of money."

The general classifications for real estate investors can be defined as follows:

1) Novice investors do less than five to six transactions per year.
2) Intermediate investors do one transaction per month or more than twelve transactions per year.
3) Advanced investors do over one hundred transactions per year.

The only difference between these three investors is speed.

NOTE: There is likely little difference in the quality of transactions between skill levels. There are many astute, careful, and slow novice investors who can earn the same or better returns then an experienced advanced investor. However, the difference between the novice and advanced is that the advanced investor does more deals, executes them faster, and utilizes opportunities to compound results.

The advanced investor is a cheetah in the jungle, and the novice is the turtle.

There is nothing wrong with being the turtle; however, the cheetah will be dominant in the market and will have access to the best opportunities and more capital due to visibility.

A problem I have had in my past businesses has been velocity. In the past, I gravitated toward slow, "residual-type" businesses.

1) One of my first businesses was as a self-employed guitar teacher where I traded my time for money. This was extremely slow because, although I had lots of clients and low overhead, it was very difficult to compound or grow this business. The residual "cash-flow-only" business model made it very hard to grow because there was never an injection of cash or credit. Every month I would take twenty-two little checks to the bank and cash them. There was never a big check that could instigate growth.

2) Another business I started in my early twenties was my debt-buying business. Debt buying is a very simple concept. Debt buyers buy charged-off, nonperforming credit cards (or other debt products) for pennies on the dollar and outsource them to collection agencies for residual income. However, this business is also a residual, cash-flow business, and it was very hard to grow this business without taking on large debt and long-term risk as well.

3) My third business was my buy-and-hold joint venture real estate portfolio. This business was great because I could joint venture with many money partners and see growth every month, but the growth and speed was linear, and again, I was seduced by the cash flow of the business and was not looking at the speed of the business. A deal would take me one whole month to find, get under contract, find a JV partner, deal with the financing, deal with the legal, take over the property, fix the problems on acquisition, show the suite to tenants, lease up, and then repeat. I became trapped in my own labor, and the velocity of this strategy kept me small. If this business were

an animal, it would be a turtle.

All of these businesses are functional: however, the businesses above are slow, cannot grow on their own cash, cannot expand easily, cannot gain any market share, and have a disproportionate amount of risk and liability when compared to the upside.

The debt-buying business and the buy-and-hold JVs also are big and clunky because they rely on debt financing and bureaucratic approval from banks, etc., to grow.

These models are slow; in fact, they're just like the heavily armored Roman legions that were destroyed by the fast-moving mounted cavalry of Attila the Hun. The Huns were fast, mobile, light, hit the battlefield by surprise, and cherry-picked the best opportunities on the field.

My new strategies do not focus on buy and hold (although I still do some buy and holds from time to time); instead I focused on three fast strategies:

    1) Wholesaling
    2) Lease options (a.k.a. rent to owns)
    3) Buy, fix, sell (retailing or flipping)

Because my goal is to have one hundred *transactions* and not hold one hundred doors at the end of the year, I must focus on fast strategies. Speed is key, and I don't want to get weighed down in a slow, long renovation or a long-term buy and hold (although these are good models).

As mentioned, three of the fastest real estate strategies (in my opinion) are wholesaling; lease options; and buy, fix, sell. However, to see the effects of choosing fast strategies, let's see the following strategies in terms of *time* so that we can compare them to the slower strategies I used to use.

    1) Wholesaling has a time frame of less than thirty days, usually seven to fourteen. It is a fast, no-debt, "no-buy" strategy that creates fast cash and fast transactions.

    2) Lease options have a time frame of less than thirty30 days to fill or set up. They are fast, can have no debt, and are a "no-buy" strategy that creates fast cash and fast transactions.

    3) Buy, fix, sell has a time frame of less than ninety days (I have

completed some buy, fix, sells in thirty days, but these shorter time frames are rare). These deals are fast, carry debt (sometimes expensive, hard money), and require capital for acquisition, but create more profits with slightly more work than wholesaling.

Every single strategy I am using can be executed within a thirty-day time frame. Time is the real currency in the market, not money. Money can be manipulated and recreated if it is lost; time is lost forever when wasted, and it is the real limiting factor in any business.

After choosing three fast, "light-on-debt-and-cash" strategies, I was confident that with the right team and systems, I could achieve my goal of one hundred transactions. It could take longer than a year, but the challenge will be met.

Chapter 32

COCA-COLA VS. DRUG DEALERS: PAY EVERYBODY

What does Coca-Cola (number fifty-nine on the Fortune 500 list of US corporations) and the multitrillion-dollar illegal drug industry have in common?

Both Coca-Cola and drug dealers have

1) Worldwide organizations
2) Highly addictive consumable products
3) Insane profit margins
4) Operations in areas where governments fail (such as war-torn zones and socially unstable areas of Africa)
5) Lineups of customers waiting to purchase a specific product who will only accept "the real thing"
6) A concentrated "producer" in both models and a large network of "distributors" (Coca-Cola makes its own syrup and hundreds of "bottling companies" distribute and bottle the mix of water and syrup.)
7) Established networks of dealers who get paid to move product

Years ago, I was watching a documentary on a war-torn country in Africa. The government had been wiped out, and it was nearly impossible to re-establish a government because of civil unrest and gangs of child armies.

Local warlords were constantly threatening any group that wished to take power, and the entire country was in chaos.

The documentary also enlightened me as to why Coca-Cola was able to operate in an environment where there was no government or regulatory body to protect their supply chains from bandits, child armies, and criminals.

One African man who worked for Coca-Cola attributed the success of the company to the fact that "everyone who touches the product gets paid." This means that everyone who carries it, sells it, distributes it, transports it, or markets it gets paid. Government protection or not, this business can function anywhere.

The multitrillion-dollar network of illegal drugs works in the same way as Coca-Cola does. These organizations face daunting odds and have gone to "war" with formidable foes like the United States Drug Enforcement Administration. However, these cartels function and thrive because they have the same philosophy driving their business:

"Everyone who touches the product gets paid."

The farmers who farm the raw materials get paid. The people who process the ingredients get paid. The drug mules get paid. The networks of dealers get paid, etc.

Coca-Cola and illegal drugs have the exact same philosophy for their supply chain and can operate anywhere in the world against all odds. Both entities have a "pay everybody" philosophy and have created an extremely smooth, well-organized, and well-oiled machine.

But what does this mean for you and your business?

Only 2 percent of business owners understand joint ventures, although most Fortune 500 companies derive significant revenues from creating joint ventures, where two companies, people, or organizations align their goals for mutual benefit.

The simplest joint ventures are referral commissions: If a customer is referred to a company, the company receiving the referral will pay an ongoing commission on all business done between the new customer and the business. This is lucrative for both the referral client and the receiving company. Ongoing revenue is what keeps the relationship strong and creates incentives for the referral client to continuously send business.

Understanding joint ventures is a huge component to becoming the leader in your market or industry. Since only 2 percent of entrepreneurs truly understand joint ventures, you can have an unfair advantage in your market.

In my own business, I have adopted a "pay everybody" policy and have had wild success with the program. I have access to private real estate deals first before they hit the open market; I have access to capital that I would not normally have access to. My phone rings all day with opportunities for deals and capital, and I don't have time to take every call—a wonderful problem to have.

Most businesses/entrepreneurs spend *huge* budgets on advertising and marketing; I spend virtually zero dollars, but I pay for results.

If someone refers me a private deal, they receive a handsome $500 "thank-you" fee. If another investor has a good deal under contract, I will generally pay $1,000 to $5,000 to purchase the contract and take on the deal myself. I have similar programs in every aspect of my business, and I don't spend any money on advertising because I pay for results, *not* promises.

In the past, I have been murdered on advertising. In 2012, I spent $2,700 on a print ad that generated only one phone call for my business (one inbound phone call and *no sale*—just a $2,700 inquiry). I was furious, felt as if I had been ripped off by the advertising company, and vowed to never ever repeat this mistake. Like the victim of a ridiculous joke, I would be extremely cautious about repeating any form of print advertising.

Nowadays, I spend zero dollars on advertising, and my phone rings off the hook because I have learned a lesson from Coca-Cola—I make sure everyone who touches my product is paid. I make sure everyone is paid well and is happy to work with me. If someone doesn't like working with me, I let him or her leave and work with someone else. I surround myself with a network of outstanding peers and highly competent people who get my phone to ring off the hook.

Unfortunately, so many entrepreneurs are too short sighted or too cheap to pay commissions to keep their people happy. This is why so many companies cannot retain good talent, spend huge dollars on advertising, and eventually become weak and vulnerable from attrition. Eventually their teams and their advertising budgets become depleted, and they have to downsize. For many businesses two of the greatest expenses are employee attrition and advertising.

Learn from Coca-Cola and drug dealers, and implement the "pay-everybody" strategy in your business. If you build a good program and stick with it, then you will see fantastic results in thirty days or less.

Chapter 33

NO-RISK PROFITS: KNOW YOUR AUDIENCE AND GIVE THEM WHAT THEY WANT

One day I was flying from Winnipeg to Chicago with a colleague of mine, and we were talking about business building; namely, flipping houses for profit. My colleague mentioned he was having trouble selling his condo that had been sitting on the market for quite some time. He initially put his condo on the Winnipeg MLS with a competent Realtor® at $120,000. The one-bedroom condo is between 400 and 500 square feet, located in downtown Winnipeg, and has no parking.

The comparables for the condo indicated that it could be sold for $120,000. Since Winnipeg is a semihot market, the Realtor® listed the condo at $99,000, hoping to get a bidding war. However, the condo has sat on the market for five months with little to no interest.

There is absolutely nothing wrong with the condo; it's cosmetically appealing, priced well, and should theoretically sell quickly on the market. However, serious buyers have avoided this condo for five months.

The price dropped from $99,000 to $95,000. Next it dropped from $95,000 to $89,900, firm. Yesterday, my colleague got an offer for $80,000, and his Realtor® was suggesting that he close at $85,000.

What went wrong with the well-priced, cosmetically appealing condo in downtown Winnipeg? It hasn't sold, even though it is priced $20,000 under comparable value.

I asked my friend if the condo had parking; he replied no. Immediately, I knew what the issue was. I asked him what the demographics were like in the building, and he said that it was composed of mostly students who take the bus to the local university.

At $99,000 or less, this condo is very well priced and a good product; however, no parking and the downtown location create two problems: 1) Downtown locations have no peripheral street parking, and 2) If the condo doesn't come with parking, there is nowhere to park the buyer's car.

People who can qualify for mortgages have jobs, which usually require cars, which require parking. No parking is a huge issue and limits the profile of buyers who would find this product attractive.

Further, the purchasing power of a person looking to buy a condo in the $100,000 to $150,000 range is too great. **There are far too many options in the condo market in Winnipeg in that price range, and a buyer can easily get a wide range of condos, with parking, in a location of their choice.**

My colleague's product is a nice product; however, his audience is very limited, and the people who would like to purchase the product (namely students) do not have the money or purchasing power to buy.

A rule I have learned in my real estate career thus far—the people who are very enthusiastic about buying usually have no money. I used to see examples of this rule all the time when I used to rent out my affordable luxury rental suites. People who were the most eager to buy had no purchasing power. Another challenge was the people who actually had cash had a wide range of options and really needed to be 100 percent happy with the product to order to buy.

To capture a person with purchasing power, you need to offer the best product at the right price and make your option the only option in the category. My friend with no parking will have a very hard time competing in his category.

When I began my business career, I would create a product I liked and would attempt to build or engineer an audience for it. This formula was extremely painful for me. I lost money numerous times and felt the defeat of failure after failure while trying to create markets for my products. Creating a market and demand for a product is very expensive, very intense, and very risky. I would not recommend it to anyone.

BUSINESS RULE: DO NOT TRY TO CREATE AN AUDIENCE. INSTEAD, FIND A PRE-EXISTING AUDIENCE WITH BUYING POWER AND GIVE THEM WHAT THEY WANT.

Today in my career, instead of creating audiences, I find audiences who are looking for specific products and offer them what they are looking for.

This subtle difference has made the difference between the failures of my past and my current successes.

For example, two years ago, rental vacancy in Winnipeg was 0.7 percent, so I built affordable luxury rental units to fill the demand. The units were quickly absorbed by the market and have been 100 percent occupied since day one. I found an audience and gave them what they wanted.

In January 2013, I noticed local investors were looking for good cash-flowing real estate deals. I made it my mission to find them deals, partnered with them, and did twelve joint ventures that year. Finding partners was easy because I filled the demand of the audience.

In the real estate investor world, I am approached weekly for mentoring and coaching, as well as speaking. I did not get into real estate to be a speaker, coach, or mentor, but I have started offering services as the demand dictates. If the audience wants coaching, I offer them coaching; if they don't want coaching, I don't offer them coaching. I absolutely hate risk, so I will not invest my time in something that people do not want.

I also noticed there is a huge audience of investors on the Internet searching for information. To feed this demand, I have provided valuable, organic blog content to the audience, and the results have been overwhelming. My blog has become a powerful marketing tool for my brand.

The lesson I have learned from my experiences is to know your audience inside and out. Know what they want, know what they don't want, and make sure you deliver at the right price. I no longer create speculative products and services because the risk is too high, and speculation is the formula for failure.

THE FORMULA FOR NO-RISK PROFITS IS VERY SIMPLE. FIND AN AUDIENCE, CONNECT WITH THEM, AND FIND OUT WHAT THEY WANT. DELIVER IT AT THE RIGHT PRICE.

You don't have to be a genius to figure out the formula above, and that's why the best entrepreneurs in the world are middle school/high school/college dropouts: business is a simple game; keep it simple.

Chapter 34

WHY FLIPPERS ARE LOSERS AND THE 15 PERCENT RULE

Flipping real estate is one of the most sensationalized forms of real estate investing around today. There are countless TV shows on television that romanticize buying distressed real estate and flipping it for profit. Although flipping real estate is one of the fastest ways to generate cash, many flippers are uneducated, unsophisticated investors who can lose their shirts if they play the game wrong.

I work with many Realtors® to find great deals to buy, fix, and sell for profit. I give the Realtors® my formula for profit and let them bring me deals. Most flipping television shows make flipping look really sexy by calculating profit like so:

(purchase price) – (renovations) = (profit)

This is how most unsophisticated, uneducated new investors calculate their profits when attempting to look for a deal to flip. However, using the formula above will absolutely kill you. Here is why:

We are missing the following: Realtor® fees, legal fees, sales discounts, financing costs, carrying costs, and insurance. For every deal that I do, I apply the 15 percent rule to it before calculating profit.

The 15 percent rule states that any buy-and-sell transaction in real estate will cost you 15 percent of the final sale price to transact. If your deal still makes sense after applying the 15 percent rule, you have a great deal.

The 15 percent is calculated using the following assumptions:

> 1) Five percent of the final sale price will go to Realtor® commissions.
> 2) Two percent of the final sale price will go to legal fees.
> 3) Three percent will go to a sales discount; we cannot assume that we sell at full price.
> 4) Five percent will go to financing, carrying, and insurance (usually this will allow for six months of carrying).
> 5) Total = 15 percent

Let's revise the "television" formula above to include the 15 percent rule:

(purchase price) – (15 percent of after repair value) – (renovations) – (profits) = (maximum allowable purchase price)

I know many of you reading this will say, *But I don't want to budget 5 percent for Realtors®; I can get my Realtor® to sell it for 4 percent!* or *I will sell it in three months instead of six months. I don't need to calculate 5 percent for carrying!* Both of those statements are true. However, the goal of the 15 percent rule is to allow for savings and impress your investors when the deal is finished. You want to give them more profit than they were anticipating rather than less. Plus, budgeting for 15 percent allows for lots of mistakes to be made in the budget, and you will still be profitable. The 15 percent rule has never let me down.

One summer I did a deal where my partner and I were planning on making $20,000 profit on a buy, fix, and sell. We used the 15 percent rule in our calculations, and we ended up making approximately $28,000 in profit instead. The 15 percent rule is brilliant because it allows for savings, and savings make everyone happy. We found savings by selling the deal privately, saving ourselves $8,000 in commissions. However, we could have sold with a Realtor® and still taken $20,000. Either way, it's a win-win scenario for everyone.

THE FIFTEEN MOST COMMON MISTAKES MADE WHEN FLIPPING REAL ESTATE

1) Buying in an area with low demand; low demand areas are very hard to sell in
2) Attempting to do renovations yourself and dragging out the project for over six months, racking up high carrying costs
3) Ordering too many custom finishes that drag out the carrying costs
4) Flipping without proper vacancy insurance, exposing you to losing all of your cash
5) Buying in a high-crime area and having the project vandalized or materials stolen
6) Modifying floor plans that end up being too costly and too risky
7) Performing electrical, plumbing, roof, or foundation repairs, which are all large-ticket items, often require permits, and are slow and expensive
8) Not paying attention to current design trends and selecting finishes that are out of style
9) Pinching pennies with the budget and underrenovating the property to the standards of the area (Tip: It is better to go over budget and have an excellent product than to stay on budget and have a substandard product. Excellent products sell fast and for top dollar.)
10) Overrenovating to standards that are far nicer than the area demands, which will kill your profits fast
11) Not offering turnkey products to the end users and failing to provide appliances (Consumers who purchase flips want turnkey products where there is nothing to do. Do not leave work for these customers; they will pay premiums to have nothing to do.)
12) Paying too much for a property or purchasing a property in a bidding war
13) Hiring an incompetent contractor
14) Selecting a property or a project that requires zoning, permits, or variances to get involved (These city departments

will drag your project out forever and can kill your profits.)

15) Forgetting about the 15 percent rule and the transaction costs of buying and selling real estate

Action Step: Analyze one hundred deals and use the 15 percent rule to determine what your maximum allowable purchase price will be. Don't forget to subtract renovations and profits. Out of one hundred deals, how many potential deals fit the formula with a realistic purchase price? From my experience, you will likely find between one and five that fit the formula.

Chapter 35

CASH FLOW DOES
NOT EQUAL PROFIT

The first deal is always the hardest deal to do. If a new investor has a good experience with their first small buy-and-hold rental house, then they keep buying more. However, in the market there are dozens of new investors who are having bad experiences—very, very bad experiences.

Cash flow is the goal of most long-term, buy-and-hold investors. Cash flow is the dream and the allure of real estate. More people get into real estate investing for the cash flow more than any other reason, and, ironically, cash flow is what makes most people leave the business as well.

When I bought my first two-bedroom, one-bath rental property and filled it with a tenant, I was very happy to receive my first income check from the property. We had great cash flow of nearly $400 at the time. Every month, after all expenses were paid, I received a check of nearly $400. As a twenty-three-year-old new investor, I felt like a genius; every month I was making a $400 profit passively, and I felt like the days of milk and honey would never end. In physics, an object that goes up must come down—it's the law of gravity and the law of the market.

After four months of $400 passive cash flow, suddenly the checks stopped coming in the mail. The tenants who had rented my house had gone delinquent, and my property manager couldn't collect. After two months of no income, the tenants skipped town and left behind a destroyed house filled with beer-stained carpets peppered with cigarette burns, trashed walls, broken doors, and bloody syringes on the floor. The cleaning lady my partners and I sent to clean up the house quit when she saw the mess, and we had to roll up our sleeves and clean it ourselves.

WHAT IS CASH FLOW?

After the house was cleaned, repaired, and filled with a new tenant under new management, the house had eaten nearly $3,000 of expenses. I had taken losses through 1) vacancy, 2) damages, and 3) normal wear and tear.

All of my cash flow profits were wiped out, and my rental property suddenly owed me money. My first instinct was, *I hate real estate, and I need to sell this house and quit this business forever!* After the house was damaged, I listed the dirty house on the market with a friend of mine who was a Realtor®, and it sat for month after month because dirty houses don't sell. Had I known about experienced investors like myself today who buy dirty houses from new investors, I would have called a "we-buy-houses" ad and would have sold the dirty house to an investor with experience—I just wanted to get out.

Cash is the lifeblood of the property, and it is not profit. Cash flow allows the property to operate, but it does not mean that the property is actually going to make money operating over time. In my experience, the maintenance and upkeep on a rental property is roughly 3 to 5 percent of the value of the property annually when every window, door, roof, cabinet, appliance, etc. is added up in value and amortized over the life of the property. For example, on my first rental house, I should have budgeted at least $250 per month just for wear and tear. I also should have budgeted 8 to 16 percent of the cash flow for vacancy because a single-family home is 8.3 percent vacant if it's vacant for one month of the year. After vacancy, damages, and normal wear and tear are accounted for, my rental house would have been making close to a $100 profit with a $400 cash flow. The lesson I learned was cash flow does not equal profit.

BUT HOW CAN YOU PROFIT FROM THIS INFORMATION?

Most real estate investors make a crucial decision on their first deal. If an investor can survive long enough to buy multiple properties, chances are they will stick around in the business until retirement. However, new investors who buy their first house; run into tenant problems; or have a dirty, damaged, and/or vacant house with slim cash flow become very motivated when they get into a cash crunch. If you can buy these "problem houses" for discounted prices or great terms, you have a chance at making a very handsome profit.

I recently bought a house from an investor who was tired of managing tenants. His property was dirty, his tenants were moving out, and it was going to be vacant. He told me he was maintaining a cash flow of $380 a month. After we did the real numbers together and added in vacancy, management, and wear and tear, he was only actually profiting $30 a month. I worked out a deal with this investor and bought his property with no money down at a low but fair price, fixed it up, and sold it in ninety days for a very nice profit.

WHERE THERE IS PAIN, THERE IS PROFIT

If I had been approached years ago on my first deal by an investor who would offer me a low but fair price for my dirty, damaged, vacant house, I would have jumped at the opportunity. I was in pain, and my pain was an opportunity for someone else to profit. I would have quit the business if I had the opportunity, but I could not find anyone to take over my problem, so instead I smartened up, expanded the business, and kept going. Every day in every market, there are new investors who absolutely hate real estate. They are in pain and want to get out of the market. Find these investors, relieve their pain, and get paid handsomely to take their pain away.

Action Step: If you own property, do a cash flow analysis of each property. Add in 3 to 5 percent of the value per year for wear and tear, a realistic vacancy budget, a management budget (even if you manage it yourself), and see if you are still maintaining a positive cash flow. If you aren't, consider using another strategy (like rent to own) on the property to gain a profit, or consider selling the property and purchasing a different property or in a different market.

Chapter 36

SINGLES VS. HOME RUNS

I have always been ambitious, and sometimes I end up biting off more than I can chew. Years ago, before I had done my first real estate deal, I read a book called *Retire in One Year* by Robin J. Elliott. The book was about using joint ventures to create enough residual income to retire in exactly one year. In the book, Robin points out that the average North American retires on an income of only $2,000 a month and that you only need $2,000 a month in passive income to retire with the same standard that most many North Americans aspire to. The idea of retiring in one year in my early twenties was absolutely alluring, and I began to focus all of my energies on doing a real estate joint venture that would provide me with $2,000 a month passive income. To go from zero dollars to $2,000 passive income with no prior experience in one year by using none of your own money is just as challenging as being able to hit a home run in baseball.

Baseball is America's favorite pastime, and America at the height of its glory was the most entrepreneurial country in the world. Baseball and entrepreneurship have many things in common, and it's natural that many baseball terms are also used in business. Terms like "third base lead" apply to leads that have been through the sales cycle but haven't become a client; this lead has rounded all the bases but has not come "home" yet. To "strike out" is to not close a sale after a presentation. My favorite baseball terms that apply to business refer to deals: A "single" is a deal that makes an acceptable amount of money with little or no risk. A "home run" is a deal that makes a larger amount of money but is rare and can have lots of risk. A "grand slam" makes such a windfall profit that your life is changed forever; however, the probability of pulling off a grand slam is extremely rare, and the risks can be high.

When I made the decision to look for a deal that could take me from zero-dollar passive income to $2,000 a month in one shot, I was swinging for a home run. The words of Donald Trump rang through my head while I was putting together my "home run": "If you're going to be thinking, you might as well be thinking big."

BABE RUTH AND THE DANGER OF THE HOME RUN

Babe Ruth was one of baseball's legends. At one time he held the world record for the most home runs. He also held the record for striking out the most times. In history, America became the most entrepreneurial country in the world because failed ventures could declare bankruptcy and allow the entrepreneur to try again. In other countries, at other points in history, failed ventures would force a failed entrepreneur into debt slavery, debtor prison, or intergenerational debt. America offered its people the option of going bankrupt instead, so a failed entrepreneur could wipe their debts clean and try again with a fresh start. In many ways, America is like baseball where you can afford to strike out over and over again and still have a chance at winning the game.

In my own business, I decided to swing for a home run at the start of my career; the payoff was high if I succeeded, but defeat would absolutely crush my investors and myself if I failed. In the process, I could potentially strike out hard and be wiped out right away.

HOW TO WIN THE WORLD SERIES

In the movie *Moneyball* with Brad Pitt, a failing major league baseball team hires a maverick baseball coach to turn the team around. The general strategy in pro baseball is to have the largest budget to buy the best players who can hit the most home runs. Home runs win games, but they are also very expensive on a team's budget. The best players who can hit home runs are naturally the most expensive players in the league and are very hard to buy if the team doesn't have an endless budget.

In *Moneyball*, the coach revolutionizes the sport of baseball with a different strategy—instead of buying home runs, which are expensive and impossible to purchase with his shoestring budget, the coach opts to buy cheaper players who are very good at hitting single bases. Although home runs are exciting to hit, you win the World Series by hitting singles, not home runs.

Although I was eventually successful with my $2,000 per month cash flow deal, my inexperience almost crushed me, and I almost went bankrupt three times before the deal became profitable. The experience was extremely valuable to my development, and today my investors are happy with their returns, but in hindsight, I would have been better off to focus on hitting many singles than swinging for a home run. The risk would have been lower, the profits could have been higher, and there would have been no chance of getting totally wiped out.

HOW I PLAY THE FIELD TODAY

Today in my business I have a very flexible approach to the market. My goal is to hit as many singles as possible. When I say "single" I mean small deals with a high degree of control that I can absolutely dominate with little effort or risk. I understand that home runs can win the game, but I also know that hitting singles wins the World Series.

I avoid focusing on one type of deal or strategy; instead, I let all types of deals come into my funnel. I sort them out like a recycling center and choose the ones that make the most money or the safest profits. If a big deal comes into my pipeline and my investors are prepared for it, I will swing for it, but only if we have proper preparation and an unfair advantage. I know that my degree of control is higher, my liquidity is better, and my risk is lower if I am doing a large volume of small deals.

WHEN TO SWITCH TO
THE MAJOR LEAGUES

The time to switch to the bigger deals and the bigger leagues is when you have far too much capital sitting on the sidelines looking for deals and you cannot deploy it all with the available deal flow in the market. Take your time in the little leagues to build your skills, build your experience, and build your brand. There will be a natural progression into bigger and more lucrative deals.

Action Step: In your business are you focusing on singles or home runs? Why have you chosen this strategy? Can you recover from failure if you "strike out"?

Chapter 37

THE $1,000 HOT DOG AND THE GENIUS BEHIND IT

One morning I was having breakfast with a colleague, and we were trying to find ways to complement each other's respective real estate businesses. Sometimes it can be difficult to find ways to complement another person's business due to personal similarities or differences, and we spent a considerable amount of time talking about our business philosophies and dreams.

My philosophy in business has predominately been: it is better to sell one $1,000 hot dog than to sell one thousand $1 hot dogs. That's why I chose to get into real estate. Instead of selling hundreds of $10 concert tickets like I used to do in my music business, I now make much more profit in real estate by only selling one item; some people would call it a $1,000 hot dog.

Selling one hot dog for $1,000 makes so much more profit, requires less effort, and has less customers and overhead than a high-volume business.

However, we don't often see any hot dog carts selling $1,000 hot dogs . . .

Why not?

Years ago on the *Celebrity Apprentice*, one of my business heroes, Gene

Simmons, sold a $5,000 hot dog to one of his friends for charity. The context of the sale was a battle between two teams of celebrities to see who could raise the most money selling hot dogs for charity. The business models of the two teams varied greatly, with one cart selling low-priced hot dogs and the other cart selling $5,000 hot dogs. The results for the two teams were were vastly different, with the low-priced hot dog making approximately $17,000, while the $5,000 hot dog made closer to $50,000.

All of the money was raised for charity, and both teams were loaded with celebrities. **Both teams did very well, but the huge difference in money raised was that one team was thinking bigger by asking for more dollars per hot dog.**

Years ago when I was in the music industry, I wanted to find a way to do business in a bigger way. Naturally, I got into real estate because in music I was selling hundreds of $1 hot dogs, whereas in real estate, I could sell a few $1,000 hot dogs and make a much better living. Real estate in general, when compared to a music business, has much better margins, takes less time and work, and is much more sustainable because there is usually only one customer instead of one thousand for a similar profit.

After I mentioned I would rather sell one $1,000 hot dog, my friend replied that his philosophy has been to sell one thousand $1,000 dogs. He elaborated by saying he was working on a multimillion-dollar land subdivision deal where he would sell nearly one hundred lots of land and, metaphorically speaking, sell one thousand $1,000 hot dogs. His thinking was clearly bigger than mine.

When we met that morning, we were looking at a house I was going to buy to flip. I had clearly illustrated my $1,000 hot dog thinking with my current business model of flipping houses one at a time. My colleague had a much greater plan to take the profits of my plan and multiply it by one hundred with the same effort.

But what do the hot dogs mean?

There are two models of how to build a business. One is vertical, and the other is horizontal.

HORIZONTAL BUSINESS— $1 HOT DOG X 1,000

A horizontal business will have lots of customers with low transaction volumes. The business relies on having a high amount of customers and transactions to make a profit. This is the hot dog cart with $1 hot dogs.

VERTICAL BUSINESS—$1,000 HOT DOG X 1

The other model is the vertical model. This model has fewer customers, but makes more money per customer. It relies on having a few fantastic customers who account for all of the business. This is the model I am building in my business today. This is the hot dog cart with the $1,000 hot dogs.

DIAGONAL BUSINESS— $1,000 HOT DOG X 1,000

There is a third model, and this model is the diagonal model that uses both vertical and horizontal strategies where we sell $1,000 hot dogs to one thousand customers. This model is much more advanced and re-quires the customer care of the vertical model with the systems and ve-locity of the horizontal model. If you can build a diagonal model, you will be rich—guaranteed. However, this model is the most difficult to create, and few people know how to actually build a diagonal business model that works.

Action Step: After examining the $1 hot dog cart and the $1,000 hot dog cart, which would you like to own? Which cart are you running in your current business? Is this where you want to be today? What is holding you back from building a diagonal business?

FINAL THOUGHTS

"Poor people spend their time to save money. Rich people spend their money to save time." —Unknown

Thank you for taking the time to invest in yourself. As Robert Kiyosaki says, "The difference between the rich and the poor is how we invest our time." In life, there is only one currency—and that is time.

The goal of this book is not only to make you money, for money is just a tool. Rather, the goal of the book is to create value by saving your limited time on this earth. If my book has helped you to decide to create wealth by becoming a real estate investor, then this book is successful. However, if my book has helped you decide you don't want to pursue real estate, then this book is successful as well.

There are many paths that lead to success and many ways to win the game of life. For me, real estate has proven to be part of my path to freedom and one of the fastest, safest, and easiest ways to wealth.

Thank you for reading,

Stefan Aarnio

ABOUT THE AUTHOR

Stefan Aarnio is one of Canada's leading up-and-coming real estate entrepreneurs and the 2012 winner of *Canadian Real Estate Wealth* magazine's Joint Venture Partner of the Year. Starting with only $1,200 cash, Stefan built a multimillion-dollar portfolio for his partners and earned himself a spot on The Self-Made List. Stefan accumulates properties at an alarming pace through his understanding of real estate joint ventures, the fastest way to acquire real estate wealth. Stefan's philosophy is simple: find great deals, build a fantastic team, pay everybody, and create partnerships for life.

EXCLUSIVE BONUSES

1) Video: "Sandman Empire—How to Create Wealth while You Sleep"
2) E-Book: *How to Start in Real Estate with Zero Dollars*
3) Video: "Build a Brand or Die a Commodity"
4) E-Book: *Double Your Income with Sandwiches and Postcards*

To claim your bonuses, go to www.MoneyPeopleDeal.com, follow the links, and use the password "insiderbonus" to access your bonus content!

MORE BOOKS BY
THE AUTHOR

What does it take to become a self-made millionaire? Many have wondered, few have succeeded. Self Made: Confessions of a Twenty Something Self Made Millionaire follows the real life story of Stefan Aarnio, award winning real estate investor and award winning entrepreneur through the struggle of starting out with zero cash, zero credit and zero experience in his pursuit of financial freedom. Inside Self Made, you will discover the 5 Secret Skills That Transform Ordinary People Into Self Made Millionaires. These skills are mastered by the rich, purposely not taught in school and are hidden from the poor and the middle class. Join Stefan on his journey as he faces financial ruin, meets his life-changing mentor and transforms his mind, body and soul to become Self Made.

Visit SelfMadeConfessions.com to order and receive your bonuses!